Peter Schreiner

Coordination, Agility, and Speed Training For Soccer

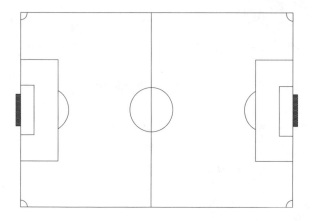

The Peter Schreiner System

Library of Congress Cataloging - in - Publication Data

by Schreiner, Peter
Coordination, Agility and Speed Training For Soccer

ISBN # 1-890946-42-7
Library of Congress Catalog Number 00-101762
Copyright © July 2000

Originally published in Germany in 2000
by Rowohlt Taschenbuch Verlag GmbH.

Art Direction
Kimberly N. Bender

Editing and Proofing
Bryan R. Beaver

Printed by
DATA REPRODUCTIONS
Auburn, Michigan

Cover Photography
EMPICS

Photography
Bongarts/Andres Rentz

Graphics
Jörg Mahlstedt

Layout
Christine Lohmann

REEDSWAIN INC
612 Pughtown Road • Spring City • Pennsylvania 19475
1-800-331-5191 • www.reedswain.com
EMAIL: info @reedswain.com

Peter Schreiner

Coordination, Agility, and Speed Training For Soccer

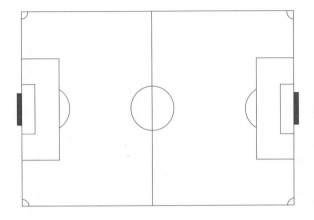

published by
REEDSWAIN INC

Table of Contents

Foreword

Viewed scientifically, coordination is the interaction of the central nervous system and the skeletal muscles in a purposeful sequence of movements.

Erich Rutemöller

Coordination is of considerable, even crucial, importance for soccer players, who find themselves in a wide variety of situations and have to perform many different movements. The highly varied situations that are encountered on a soccer pitch are factors that make the sport so popular and unusually attractive to young and old, as active players or spectators.

A book such as Peter Schreiner's is long overdue and I am pleased and grateful that he has dealt with this subject at last. In his previous activities and publications, Peter has shown that his theoretical knowledge and many years of practical experience make him the ideal author to describe complex themes systematically, relevantly and simply. This is enormously helpful for the many coaches and teachers who are seeking a practical guide for their training sessions.

Peter Schreiner covers the spectrum from general coordination conditioning to soccer-specific coordination conditioning with great conviction, making clear the highly important link between technique and coordination.

German players at both junior and senior levels are often criticized, sometimes too readily and on superficial grounds, for their poor coordination. This is certainly true when they are compared with their South American or African counterparts.

Coaches and teachers at all age and performance levels should make use of every opportunity to carry out consistent coordination conditioning to systematically develop and improve the innate skills and existing potential of their players. They will find this book to be an excellent aid.

I wish soccer coaches and teachers lots of fun when they use the many interesting drills described and presented here by Peter Schreiner with his usual clarity.

Erich Ruthemöller
German Soccer Association coach

Introduction

Coordination

One of the subjects I dealt with during my sports studies was, of course, coordination conditioning. I did not follow it up, however, and it was only later that I recognized the special importance of coordination conditioning for all athletes.

How did I come to recognize this? In 1995, when I was responsible for organizing a basic conditioning program for the German soccer club FC Schalke 04, I developed a concept for teaching creative attacking techniques. In 1996, while I was involved in this project, I met Dirk Rauin, a former international team handball player, who regularly rounded off basic conditioning sessions with coordination conditioning drills. The young players of Schalke 04 were able to profit from his experience as a team handball coach, supplemented by ideas on coordination and speed conditioning derived from the extremely successful youth coaching work of the Dutch soccer club Ajax Amsterdam. Rauin systematically extended the content of the basic coordination conditioning and I introduced soccer elements into his collection of drills. In 1997 we marketed this new concept in the form of two videos – "Coordination, Agility, and Speed Training For Soccer". In the course of my editorial supervision of this video project I had taken a more intensive look at coordination conditioning for soccer players.

In 1997, at the International Coaches Congress of the Association of German Soccer Teachers, we presented the basic coordination conditioning of FC Schalke 04 in the Mungersdorfer stadium in Cologne with great success.

This book

In January 1998 I attended the Soccer Convention of the NSCAA (National Soccer Coaches Association of America) in Cincinati, Ohio. I wanted to see how professional Americans organize such a large-scale coaching event with 4500 participants. At the same time I was able to visit Reedswain Soccer Videos and Books, the publisher of our videos on the Peter-Schreiner-System and Coordination Conditioning and answer questions from interested American coaches at Reedswain's booth. I was overwhelmed by the warmth and enthusiasm of the Americans, and was able to see for myself that the videos were selling very well. Many coaches asked when the books to the videos would be available, thus providing an added stimulus for me to write this book.

Collection of drills

In many of my soccer seminars in recent years I found that coaches regarded the photocopies of the demonstrated drills as very important, and they were absolutely necessary for the execution of the drills during training sessions. Coaches and teachers showed increasing interest in an easily understood coaching guide with a systematic collection of drills on the subject of coordination. This interest was not restricted to coaches of junior teams. More and more "senior" coaches attended my seminars and tested the drills with adult players of all levels of ability. I was gratified by the many comments and suggestions I received. This is therefore a suitable place to express my thanks to all coaches and teachers who tested my drills, reported back to me about their experience, and suggested variations and extensions. Dirk Rauin, Peter Hyballa, Dirk Reimöller, Lothar Jahn, Heinrich Schmidt, Martin Möllmeier, Achim Nohlen, Phillip Senge and Gerd Thissen all deserve special mention. They helped me to expand my collection of drills while making it more soccer-specific. The numerous general coordination drills were complemented by growing numbers of drills designed specifically for soccer players. I would also like to thank the women's team of FCR Duisburg, the players of TuS Bochum-Hordel and, in particular, my students Patrick Dehn and Sascha Schneider, who have demonstrated the drills in photos and video sequences over the years.

Workbook and easily understandable guide for coaches and teachers

This book is intended as a practical guide rather than a scientific treatise on coordination. Nevertheless, for those who are interested, the principles of coordination conditioning are explained at the start of the book. The extensive drills section is organized by subject. The organizational forms and the drills themselves are shown and described clearly and understandably. Any coach can use this book as a workbook and quickly find what he needs within the different subjects.

Most coaches want tried and proven drills augmented by useful tips and understandable instructions and descriptions. You will find all of these in this book. You do not need to read the book page for page from front to back. Pick out the drills that appeal to you most or are of interest for the group you coach, and incorporate them into your coaching sessions. When you have the time you should also read the basic information and methodical tips, so that you gain the necessary background knowledge to get the most out of the organizational forms. The numerous photos are intended to make the sometimes difficult movements and sequences clearer. One picture says more than a thousand words. In general, the emphasis has been on clear descriptions and ease of understanding.

Soccerobics

I would like you to draw your attention to Soccerobics in particular. This combination of ball, coordination and music opens up new opportunities in coordination conditioning, which you should certainly try out.

The many Soccerobics demonstrations for the Association of German Soccer Teachers, the German Soccer Association and a number of its regional associations, The Coaches Super Clinic in America, as well as seminars with coaches and teachers, have aroused considerable interest. Reactions were overwhelmingly favorable and stimulated a demand for further information. In view of the great enthusiasm, especially among children, and the many and varied conditioning effects, Soccerobics should be given a chance.

Use new ideas

Experience has shown that, in the absence of special training, inexperienced coaches and teachers in particular are reluctant to include new ideas into their coaching sessions. They rely on tried and trusted methods. This inhibits the further development of coaching methods and ideas. I hope that this book will encourage the many coaches and especially teachers to try out the drills described in it and to incorporate them in their coaching and instruction. I would also like coaches at all levels of soccer to look into coordination conditioning more deeply and pass on the benefits to their players.

Coaches should familiarize themselves with the difficult movements, but no soccer player will expect his coach to be able to demonstrate every movement to perfection. A description of a drill often suffices. The players will usually be quick to translate it into practice.

I hope that this book helps to widen and systematize the coaching of soccer players and that it will provide coaches at all levels with stimulating new ideas for varied and exciting coordination conditioning.

Peter Schreiner

Coordination - a key skill

The fascination of stars

Why do we still remember certain soccer players years after we saw them? What makes them legendary? One thing is clear; soccer idols are not remarkable for their outstanding physical condition. Other traits make an average soccer player into a star. Franz Beckenbauer, Johan Cruyff, Pelé and other exceptional soccer players had a high level of soccer intelligence and extraordinary technique, as do the stars of today. These players certainly have and had a good conditional basis, but over and above this they were able to:
- analyze game situations correctly in a split second, in other words to read the game;
- make clever tactical decisions quickly;
- put their tactical decisions into effect with their outstanding technical capabilities.

What skills does a star need?

To be able to exploit his ability to read the game and his vision and anticipation, a player needs a perfect "feel" for the ball (ability to control and run with the ball, timing, ability to strike a perfectly weighted pass into free space), so that he does not have to focus his attention on the ball all the time. Spectacular tricks round off the picture and create situations that bring spectators to their feet in admiration. Above-average powers of observation are the basis for speed of reaction, even in complex situations. In other words, exceptional soccer players have outstanding coordination skills.

Necessity for extra coaching

Why has coordination conditioning become so important in modern soccer? One reason is that the world of children has changed dramatically in recent decades.
- They no longer spend much time climbing, rolling, hopping, jumping and balancing.
- Children often do not get enough exercise and they consequently have coordination deficits.

These shortcomings should be compensated for by teachers in their schools and soccer coaches in their clubs.

Coordination conditioning and top soccer

Not every child can be a star. However, systematic and competent coaching of young players should create the broad basis that is needed to give the most talented ones the opportunity to develop their full potential. Everyone knows about Ajax Amsterdam, but German professional clubs such as FC Schalke 04 have also provided general and soccer-specific coordination conditioning for their young players for many years. They have recognized that coordination skills are an important precondition for performing well at the top level.

General and varied coordination conditioning should be part of the basic education of young soccer players, but players of all ages and levels of ability can benefit from supplementary coordination drills. The core aspects and objectives depend on the players' abilities and the age structure of the group. While 9-year-olds need varied movement drills of a general coordinative nature, top soccer players should make use of their soccer techniques in coordination training sessions under a variety of conditions (e.g. under pressure of time or in tight situations).

Coordination Conditioning

Coordination as the basis of success

Several muscles are needed to enable the body to perform soccer movements properly, quickly, powerfully and enduringly. The muscles of soccer players should therefore be controlled by a finely tuned nervous system. The exact coordination of skeletal muscles and central nervous system is regulated and controlled by bodily processes that are covered by the term "coordination". Coordination is, however, a multifaceted term. In essence it relates to learning, controlling and using movements. Soccer players should be capable of learning new techniques quickly, economically and precisely, and adjusting them to take account of unexpected events. Players who have been taught good coordination can control their movements when they have to act quickly, under pressure from an opponent, in tight situations.

Coordination skills

Before we deal with conditioning for coordination skills we should take a close look at the following questions.

- Are there coordination skills that are needed for all types of sports and sporting tasks?
- Are reaction times in athletics and soccer and in reaction tests with electronic machines all dependent on one and the same skill?
- Is, for example, the ability to balance on a board that is supported by a ball of any relevance to the demands made on a soccer player's sense of balance?

Experts have expressed justified doubts about whether there are skills that can be conditioned independently of a specific type of sport. The complex reactions of a soccer player depend on a host of perceptive elements and previous experience (anticipation). They certainly cannot be compared with the reaction to a simple signal such as a starter's pistol. This is why coordination skills should not be worked on in isolation from the circumstances and demands of the type of sport.

Which coordination skills are important for a soccer player?

- Spatial orientation (i.e. a player's awareness of his own position on the pitch in relation to teammates and opponents, even after turning).
- Kinesthetic differentiation (e.g. "feel" for the ball).
- Balance (e.g. stable posture even when under pressure from an opponent).
- Speed of reaction (e.g. to be able to be first to the ball when it rebounds from the goalkeeper)
- Rhythmic skills (e.g. an explosive start on landing after jumping to head the ball, or an elegant dribble after a feint).

The following coordination skills are often mentioned in the literature, but are not dealt with in detail here.

- Motor adjustment.
- Combinatory ability.
- Sense of movement.
- Suppleness.
- Anticipation.
- Motor memory.

Coordination conditioning in soccer

How can all of these skills and components be taught and conditioned? What are the consequences for training sessions with soccer players? Movement coordination contains a high proportion of perception, anticipation and concentration.

Soccer players should carry out general coordination drills as early as possible, so that they can learn to move their bodies precisely in a wide variety of ways. The more varied a soccer player's childhood experience of movement, the better he can control his muscles with the help of his nervous system. Numerous drills can be found in the appropriate chapter on "General coordination conditioning" starting on page 16. Coaches should always remember that coordination conditioning is "not stereotyped, dull or distracting repetition of movements but is a motivated, concentrated and varied movement activity."

As young soccer players become older and their skills improve, the proportion of soccer-specific coordination conditioning should be increased. The typical demands that the game makes on the player should be at the heart of coordination conditioning. It is important that varied basic conditioning with general coordination drills for soccer players should be followed by effective coordination conditioning with soccer-specific movements (techniques) under varying conditions of difficulty. In concrete terms this means that the players should be asked to use techniques that they have already mastered while carrying out additional tasks under more difficult or changed conditions. The coach could place rods or tires in sequence and ask the players to run over them before or after using soccer techniques, or he could ask the players to perform drills within a certain time. This subject is dealt with in detail in the chapter on "Special coordination conditioning for soccer players," starting on page 85.

To summarize, coordination is a key skill for success in soccer and should therefore be given high priority in training sessions.

GENERAL COORDINATION CONDITIONING

Coordination Conditioning

Coordination and the nervous system

Soccer players should learn as early as possible to move their bodies precisely in a wide variety of ways. The more varied their childhood experience of movement, the better they can control their muscles with the help of the nervous system. "Young players with good coordination can perform better at soccer than others who have the same or even slightly better conditional potential. Only soccer players with well developed coordination skills can translate their conditional capabilities optimally into corresponding performances."

Running coordination for soccer players

Modern soccer is characterized by its high tempo. To play soccer successfully, players must react faster than ever when they receive the ball, as well as making frequent sudden changes of direction, sprints into free space and instant switches from defense to attack. The demands on soccer players are so great that special and systematic training of their running coordination, especially their running technique and rhythm, appears essential.

What are the special aspects of the conditioning of running coordination for soccer players? The running performance demanded of a soccer player differs considerably from that of an athlete. Sprints, turns, changes of direction, runs with the ball and challenges for the ball both before and after a sprint require the player to adjust his stride length and frequency to widely varied game situations. This makes a variable, flexible and selective application of running techniques during the game necessary.

For selective conditioning of running coordination, it is necessary to set priorities within training sessions. Fast footwork, involving lightning fast coordination of nerves and foot muscles, is at the heart of many drills. Small, rapid steps ensure that the player can control the ball securely and move in any direction he chooses. The object is to remain in contact with the ground. He can then retain control of his body and accelerate quickly in any given direction. In addition, good footwork is essential to a good shooting technique. By continuously adjusting his distance from the ball, a player ensures that he is in the best position when he shoots.

As a result of practicing changes in stride frequency and length in a variety of drills, a player is able to adjust his speed to the needs of the game situation. A long, powerful sprint down the wing requires a different technique to a subtle change of direction and a short sprint in a restricted space. Players should also be able to switch smoothly and quickly from the small strides appropriate to a challenge for the ball to the long strides needed to sprint away into space.

Coordination and strength

In this chapter you will find drills with one-footed and two-footed "rebound" jumps. The combination of jumping and running has a prominent place in general coordination conditioning.

Soccer players should be able to combine running and jumping movements rhythmically with soccer techniques without losing their balance. In soccer a short, explosive acceleration is often decisive for the success of a run with the ball. This is closely bound up with the strength of the leg muscles. It should be possible to activate all parts of each individual muscle in a well-coordinated manner, to utilize all of their potential strength and energy. This intra-muscular coordination is reflected in a player's ability to develop his maximal strength and speed to the fullest. The inter-muscular coordination of the measured contraction of one set of muscles (agonists) and the simultaneous opposing contraction of another set (antagonists) is also crucial to a player's speed, strength and endurance.

Coordination and endurance

Economical use of the muscles participating in a movement (e.g. running) and the simultaneous relaxation of the non-participating muscles results in energy-saving soccer activity. Improvement of intra-muscular and inter-muscular coordination thus has a direct effect on a player's endurance.

Coordinative Warm-up

Players' warm-up routines should contain easy coordination tasks. These might be drills to improve their running technique (see page 72) or their running coordination, or unusual ways of running with one or more balls. Training sessions for young players and teenagers should always contain dribbling games, which promote improvement of general coordination skills as well as being a lot of fun.

Coaches should vary the form and content of warm-up sessions to ensure that their players remain motivated. The more variation, the more successful the coaching, especially with regard to coordination.

Two organization forms have proved their value in the coaching of young players and adults:
- "Zipper"
- Running round a square

There are also a number of interesting drills for pairs of players.

"ZIPPER"

Motivational warm-up should be fun, should prepare the players for the main part of the training session, and should contain coordination tasks. The "zipper" is an excellent framework for varied warm-up. It gives the coach plenty of opportunities for combining running coordination drills with ball drills. This improves the players' ability to perform actions with and without the ball and to adjust their running speed to the speed of their teammates.

The drills can focus on two aspects.

- On the longer sides of the area the players can carry out individual tasks with and without the ball.
- On the diagonals the players can carry out typical "zipper" drills.

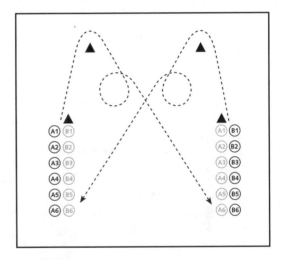

The "zipper": an ideal framework for coordinative warm-up.

On the long sides of the area

Drills without a ball. Various drills for improving running technique (see page 72) ensure intensive warm-up and make demands on the players' coordination skills.

- Slowly bend the knee and draw up the heel backward as far as it will go
  - right and left leg alternately
  - only the right leg, taking one or two steps after each bend
  - only the left leg, taking one or two steps after each bend
- As above, but faster

- Running and bending the ankles
  - on the spot
  - over a short distance
- Hopping
- Sidesteps
- Running and raising the knees high
- Skipping (fast leg movement, knee raised to the horizontal)
  - both legs
  - only right or left leg, taking one or two steps after each skip
  - the stork (skips with emphasis on lower leg movement)
- Raise knees; arms stretch out forward horizontally
- Cross steps (only forward or forward and backward alternately)

Drills with the ball. The players in the group adjust their speed to maintain the correct distance from each other. The coach dictates the tempo. The first player in the group has to maintain the specified tempo and observe the leading player of the other group. Both ensure that the two groups arrive in the middle at the same time and thread their way through each other.

Turns prior to passing through the other line of players improve the players' sense of orientation and their ability to keep at a constant distance from each other by maintaining the same speed. Drills carried out in pairs in the center involve contact and transition phases.

- Running and throwing the ball into the air and catching it
- Bouncing the ball
  - with the right hand
  - with the left hand
  - alternately
- Running with the ball on the ground
  - with the right foot
  - with the left foot
  - with alternate feet, with a ball contact after each stride
- Running with the ball, using the inside of the foot
- Scissor, step-over, dummy step with two intermediate steps

On the diagonal sides

Individual drills without the ball. The coach tells the players how to move (e.g. run forward, run backward, hop, sidestep, raise your knees, skip). The degree of difficulty can be increased by asking the players to carry out additional tasks such as turns and jumps before the two lines cross.

Fast turn. Each player in the two intersecting lines maintains a constant distance from the player in front of him. When a player is about 2 yards from the middle, he quickly makes a complete rotation before running through the point of intersection with the other line.

This fast rotation conditions the players' sense of orientation. After making the rotation the player must quickly correct his distance from the player in front and adjust his speed to that of the players in the other line.

Fast rotation before reaching the middle

Drills with a partner. The players can carry out drills with a partner at the center of the square. Examples include "clashing chests," high fives (with one or both hands), and passing the ball from hand to hand or foot to foot or combinations of both. These drills improve the players' sense of orientation and their timing.

Soccer players should be able to land securely and continue running after jumping. When two players jump up and towards each other, making contact in the air before landing and running, this is not only a lot of fun but also conditions the players' coordination skills.

Clashing chests

Clapping hands in the center. The players run two by two into the center and clap hands (one or both) with each other. They then run on, each in his line, to the next cone.

High fives in the center

Drills with a ball. When the players in the two lines dribble a ball, they have to take care to maintain their distance from the player in front and stay in step with the players in the other line. To do this they have to look up from the ball and adjust their speed if necessary.

- Carry a ball and hand it over in the center (group A players have a ball, group B players do not).
- Dribble a ball (each player has a ball; the two lines simply thread through each other in the center).
- Dribbling with a rotation before crossing through the other line.
- Transfer the ball with the foot (group A players have a ball, group B players do not).
- Double transfer (group A players dribble a ball, group B players carry one).
- At the center the group A players pick up the ball and carry it, while the group B players put the ball on the ground and dribble with it.

"Zipper" with dribbling

Ball transfer on the ground

Ball transfer with feet and hands. When two players cross in the center, one hands over the ball to the other and the other passes the ball from foot to foot. A lot of concentration is required to do this smoothly and cross over in the center without stumbling.

Ball transfer in the air and on the ground

RUNNING IN THE SQUARE

"Running in the square" is another form of organization for motivational coaching of large groups. The players stand at each corner of a 15 yard x 15 yard square. Two or four players set off at the same time, run to the center of the square, carry out a task, then run to the end of the line of players at the opposite corner.

- The first players in group A and group C start at the same time and run to the center. When they reach the center, the first players of groups B and D set off, and so on. The players run straight across the square and join the back of the group at the opposite corner.
- The first players of groups A and C set off as before but turn through 90 degrees at the center instead of running straight across the square.

Variation: Before they turn, the players make one complete clockwise rotation.

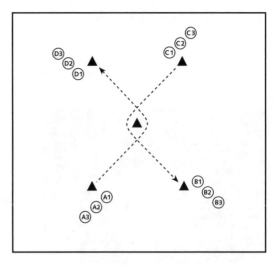

Diagonal runs in the square (pairs of players)

Four-player start. In this drill the first players of all four groups start together, meet in the center and turn simultaneously through 90 degrees.

Variation: Before they turn, the players make one complete clockwise rotation.

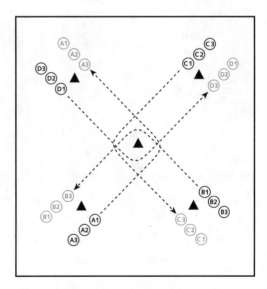

Four-player start: The first players of all four groups start together

TWO-PLAYER DRILLS

Two-player warm-up drills are very popular.
Zig-Zag. The players have to coordinate a given change of pace.

Zig-zag: Jog to the middle, run to the outside

Sidesteps with arm movements. Sidesteps while carrying out arm movements in parallel (e.g. high fives and low fives), to coordinate the speed and precision of the body movements.

Sidesteps: High fives and low fives

Running and jumping

The drills in this chapter are characterized by organization forms and aids (rods, cones and tires). These are the framework for numerous movement drills for general coordination conditioning.

No limits are placed on the coach's creativity. Tires and rods can be combined in lots of different ways, so running and jumping drills need never be boring.

DRILLS WITH RODS

Railroad track

The simplest organization form for general coordination conditioning is the "railroad track," made of parallel rods. Depending on the size of the group and the coaching objectives, 1 to 3 tracks can be set up so that the players do not have to wait too long for their turn.

- 30 players can carry out running or simple jumping drills on three tracks without any difficulty.
- Experience shows that even players who dislike running enjoy these drills.
- Just one track is often sufficient for a soccer team, especially if another activity has to be carried out immediately after finishing the track.
- The coach should stand beside the track so that he can give instructions or demonstrate what he wants the players to do and immediately correct any mistakes.

7 to 10 rods are placed parallel to each other at intervals of around 2 feet, resting on the ground or on small or large cones.
- The length of the players' legs and the activities they have to carry out must be taken into consideration when deciding on the distance between rods.
- The distance should be varied constantly.
- *Important:* The players should start the running drills by leading with the left leg as well as the right.

The degree of difficulty can be varied, depending on the length of the players' legs.
- *Height of the rods or cones:* Beginners and young players up to 8 years old should carry out the drills with the rods on the ground. Advanced and older players should practice with the rods at different heights.
- *Speed of execution:* The more familiar the players become with the railroad track, the faster they should carry out the drills.
- *Activities:* The more complex and unusual the activity, the more is required of the players.
- *Distractions:* While the players are learning to carry out the activities on the track, some players might distract the others with arm movements and/or shouts.

Ways of running
- Forward: 1 ground contact
- Forward: 2 ground contacts
- Sideways: 1 ground contact
- Sideways: 2 ground contacts
- Backward: 1 ground contact
- Backward: 2 ground contacts
- Hopping
- Cross steps, front
- Cross steps, front and behind alternately

Additional arm movements. Running over the railroad track is more difficult if the players cannot use their arms to give stability by adjusting them to the rhythm of the run. The players should therefore carry out the runs with their arms in a variety of positions.

- Arms at their sides
- Arms held out straight at shoulder height
- Arms held out straight forward
- Arms behind their backs
- Movements with the arms (e.g. boxing movements)

Running with the arms out straight at shoulder level

Skipping sideways. Fast sideways steps while vigorously raising the knees can be carried out with two or more ground contacts. The players should land lightly on the balls of their feet rather than stamping. As a new activity, the players can start with the right or left foot.

Note: The players always start with the foot that is closest to the rod. The coach should switch from one side of the track to the other and ask the players to turn to face him. They will then automatically start with the correct foot.

- Start with the left foot
- Start with the right foot
- Change of direction: three rods forward, one back
- Change of direction: two rods forward, one back

Skipping sideways with two ground contacts

Running backward. Situations arise in every game where the players have to run backward and simultaneously observe the game situation. In this drill the players run backward without touching the rods, while looking over their shoulder to see where they are going.

Running backward while looking over the shoulder

Slalom. The rods are ideal for carrying out slalom runs with short fast sidesteps.

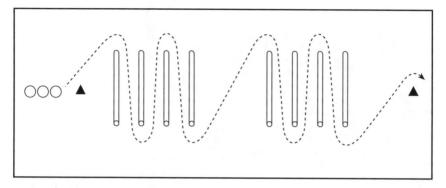

Cross steps. The rear leg, which is pointing in the direction of the forward movement, can cross either only in front of the other leg or alternately in front and behind.

Cross steps. Take the front leg across the back leg and into the next gap between the rods.

Variation: Holding and moving the arms in different ways increases the level of difficulty.

Cross steps: Arms held out to the side at shoulder level; arms held in the air

Two-footed bouncing jumps

Two footed bouncing jumps. The players should "bounce" from gap to gap with minimal ground contact. They should land lightly on the balls of their feet.

Variations
- Bouncing forward: 2 ground contacts/1 ground contact
- Bouncing backward: 2 ground contacts/1 ground contact
- Bouncing sideways: 2 ground contacts/1 ground contact
- Bouncing sideways: 1 ground contact/rod between the feet
- Bouncing jumps: 3 forward/1 backward
- Bouncing forward: 1 ground contact/ arms held sideways, forward or in the air

One-footed bouncing jumps. One-footed bouncing jumps put a lot of strain on the ankles and knees and should only be practiced if the players have sufficiently well developed muscles. A change of jumping foot is advisable. Under no circumstances should too many jumps be carried out with one foot.

One-footed bouncing jumps

Combinations of one- and two-footed bouncing jumps. Alternating one- and two-footed bouncing jumps is rhythmically difficult.
- left foot, both feet, right foot, both feet, etc.
- left foot, left foot, both feet, right foot, right foot, both feet, etc.

Hopping. Some soccer players find hopping difficult. When they have to hop over the railroad track they have problems maintaining the correct rhythm. When the players have mastered the rhythm, the coach should ask them to swing their arms vigorously.

Hopping while swinging the arms vigorously

Groups of two

Groups of two can also practice on the railroad track. One player gives the start signal and the two of them try to synchronize their movements as they proceed along the track.

Activities
- Run straight over the track (e.g. sidesteps, cross steps)
- Hopping (two-footed sideways hopping)
- Change of direction:
  - the coach specifies the steps and the players try to carry them out synchronously
  - one player signals a change of direction and the other tries to follow precisely and quickly
- After the last rod the players can carry out another activity
  - a sprint immediately after crossing the last rod
  - a sprint at a signal from a player
  - a turn and sprint
  - a sprint and a shot at goal

Groups of two on the railroad track

Variation: Small reaction games can be carried out. One player can signal when a change of direction has to be made as the players proceed along the track. The following two players must leave a sufficient gap or each group must have its own small track.

Arranging the rods or small hurdles

It is important to create variable conditions for coordination drills. This means that the coach should constantly vary the distances and arrangement of the rods in the railroad track. He might use the following variations.

Uniform change of distance between rods. All of the rods are 18 inches apart initially. After a time the distance can be changed to 24 inches, or a second track can be set up with this distance. If enough rods are available a number of tracks can be set up. Constant changes from track to track are good for practicing running with frequent changes of stride length.

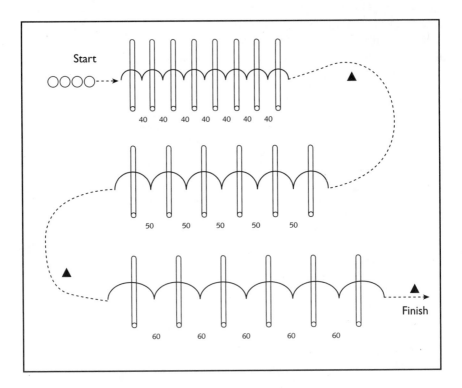

Dynamic change of distance between rods. The distance between the first rods is 18 inches and is increased at intervals of 6 inches until it is so wide that the players can just cope.

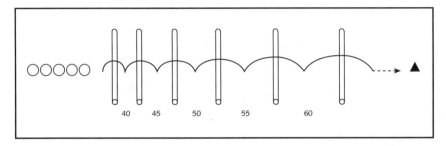

Larger distance for interim steps. The distance between the small hurdles can be chosen so that the players constantly have to adjust their stride length between successive hurdles (in the same way as hurdlers). The number of possible steps obviously depends on the distance between the hurdles. During a drill with equally spaced rods, the coach should require the players to make different numbers of steps, so that they always have to adjust. If the number of steps is even and then uneven, there is a change of leading foot.

- Sequence of steps: right - two - three - four - right - two - three - four - right - etc.
- Sequence of steps: right - two - three - left - two - three - right - two - three - left - etc.

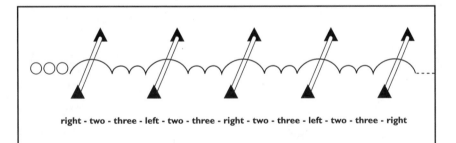

right - two - three - left - two - three - right - two - three - left - two - three - right

Alternating sequences of high and low hurdles. At regular intervals higher hurdles (12 inches) can give way to lower hurdles (6 inches) or rods and vice versa.

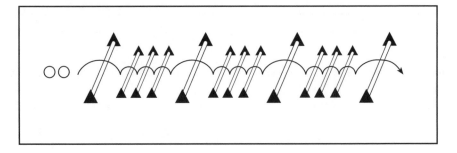

Railroad track with gaps. If the rods are arranged with gaps of 5 to 7 yards the coach can ask the players to carry out additional activities in these gaps.

Additional activities in the gaps

Turn in the middle. Turn once to the right and once to the left.
- Complete rotation (360 degrees) then continue forward
- Half turn (180 degrees) then continue backward

Turn in the middle

Sprint to the cone. Turn to the outside, run to the outside cone and touch it, then run back to the middle and continue down the track (here: side-steps). This basic drill can be expanded with other activities.
- Run to cone on the right or left after a hand signal or a call
- Turn quickly through 270 degrees and run to the cone

Sprint to outside cone

Zigzag sprint between the hurdles. Fast sequences of steps over the hurdles can be supplemented by a zigzag sprint - a very important element of soccer. The players can touch the cone with a hand or foot or turn through 180 degrees.

OTHER ARRANGEMENTS OF RODS

Combination of rods across and along the track

Greater variation can be introduced by using this combination of rods lying across the track and along it. 2 to 5 rods lie across the track, about 24 inches apart. In the center are 2 to 3 rods pointing along the track. Finally there are another 2 to 5 rods across the track.

Jumping and running drills

- Faster zigzag run
- Fast zigzag bouncing jumps forward
- Sidesteps forward
- Sprint (rod between feet)
- Bouncing jumps (rods between feet)

Double rods along the track

Double rods can be laid along the track, making other additional activities possible.

Jumping and running drills

- Faster zigzag run
- Fast zigzag bouncing jumps forward

Variable arrangement of rods

The arrangement of rods across and along the track, also in combination with gaps (and later with tires) offers lots of opportunities for variations. No limits are imposed on the coach's creativity. In this arrangement, for example, two-footed and one-footed bouncing jumps can be combined with sideways skips. The first player starts on the left, the next on the right, and so on.

Distractions

Distractions such as arm movements and noise can be used to make the players concentrate harder during general coordination drills.

Railroad track with distractions

Individual drills with rods

This section describes drills for single players with one or more rods. The players do not run over a railroad track but have their own drill area and their own activities to carry out.

Note: 2 or 3 cones in a row can be used instead of a rod, if insufficient rods are available.

Single rod

Definitions: Sidesteps are steps to the side, making full contact with the ground and transferring the full weight of the body to the take-off foot. A tap is a brief foot contact with the ground, without transferring weight to the foot. Increasing the height of the rod increases the degree of difficulty.

Running and jumping drills

- Short turns (like skiers)
- Sidesteps (with and without taps)
- Crossover jumps

Crossover jump: take-off stance

Crossover phase: airborne phase

Two parallel rods

Two parallel rods present new variation opportunities. The players start on one side and carry out the movements specified by the coach (e.g. sidesteps). The distance between the rods can be varied, as well as the height of the rods.

Sidesteps over two parallel rods.

Sidesteps with tap. Drills that combine sideways stopping movements and step sequences are very important for soccer players. The players learn to stop suddenly when moving sideways and continue the movement in the opposite direction. This is especially important for feints (as an attacker or defender).

The player makes sidesteps between two parallel rods, finishing with tap steps. He starts with the leg closest to the first rod.

Sequence of steps: left, right - left, tap (back), right, left - right, tap (back), etc. The change of direction should be as smooth as possible.

Sidesteps with tap

Variations
- As above, but placing the full weight on the foot when changing direction rather than making a tap step.
- Sequence of steps: left, right - left, right (do not put the right foot to the ground) (back) right, left - right, left (do not put the left foot to the ground) (back) and so on
- Two-footed bouncing jumps (2 ground contacts/1 ground contact) sideways over the rods. The contact with the ground should be brief. The players should be relaxed - not tense - as they land lightly on the balls of the feet.
- One-footed bouncing jumps (2 ground contacts/1 ground contact). Take care: This puts a lot of strain on the ankles - only suitable for experienced players.

- Combinations/changes: sidesteps and jumps
  Sequence of steps: left, right - left, tap (back), right, left - right, tap,
  then two-footed bouncing jumps to the left and back, then sidesteps
  again, and so on.
- Other variations can be used with the arms held in different positions
  (arms held out sideways, to the front, straight up).

Three parallel rods

Three parallel rods offer more opportunities for variation and a longer
sequence of steps.

Each set of three rods can be used by two or three players in turn. This
ensures that the players have sufficient rest. In addition the players can
encourage and correct each other. When the players are sure of the step
sequences they can gradually increase their speed, while still carrying out
the steps precisely.

Example: Sidesteps with two ground contacts and tap steps after the
last rod. The player starts with the foot that is closest to the first rod.
Sequence of steps: 1, 2-1, 2-1, tap (back), 1, 2-1, 2-1, tap and so on.

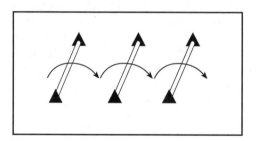

Variations: All variations from the first railroad track can be used. In addition, cross steps and step-overs can be introduced:
The players start with the foot that is furthest away from the rod.
Sequence of steps: cross, 2 cross, tap (back), cross, 2 cross, 2 cross, tap and
so on.
Note: It is important to be near the rod when starting a cross step, so that
there is enough space for the second step. After the tap step behind the
last rod, the steps are repeated in the reverse direction.

Four parallel rods

The drills with three rods can also be carried out over four or five rods. The number of variation options is even greater. Changes of direction can be made (e.g. two sidesteps, one sidestep with tap backward, then continue in the initial direction).

Sequence of steps: left, right - left, tap - right (back), tap - left, right - left, tap - right (back), tap - left, right - left, tap and so on in the same way backward.

Diagonal rods

Running and jumping drills
• Hopping forward and backward
• Alternate step and jump
• Run (two ground contacts) forward and backward

Diagonal rods: alternate step and jump

DRILLS WITH HOOPS

Hoop track
Hoops can be quickly arranged to form a variety of tracks. The hoops should have a diameter of 24 to 30 inches. The coach can ask the players to carry out running and jumping sequences to improve their coordination.

Running and jumping drills
- One ground contact
- Two ground contacts
- Forward with a change of direction (e.g. three hoops forward and one backward)

Coordinated running on a hoop track: running with two ground contacts in each hoop.

Coordinated jumping on a hoop track: two-footed bouncing jumps

Additional arm movements
- Arms against thighs
- Arms held out to the side
- Arms held into the air
- Arm movements for using chest expanders or clapping hands
- Shadow boxing with right and left fist in turn

- Lift each arm in turn from the thigh until it is stretched out horizontally
- Arm movements like a Jumping Jack
- Arm movements like a Jumping Jack in reverse

More ideas for Jumping Jack movements can be found on page 61 under "Arm and leg coordination."

Change of arms. Opening and closing the legs (Jumping Jack) is combined with lifting and lowering the arms. Only when the players can carry out the leg movements automatically will they be able to carry out this variation correctly.

Change of arm and leg movements

OTHER ARRANGEMENTS OF HOOPS

Basic arrangement 1-2-1-2-1-2-1

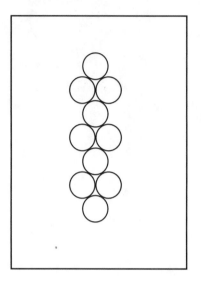

The basic arrangement of hoops for coordination drills over a hoop track consists of alternate single and double tires. This is ideal for the jumping sequence, opening and closing the legs, but is also suitable for a variety of running and jumping drills.

Running and jumping drills
- Jumps: open - close
- Runs, 1 ground contact in each hoop
- Runs, 2 ground contacts
- Two-footed bouncing jumps, 2 forward, 1 backward

Cross track

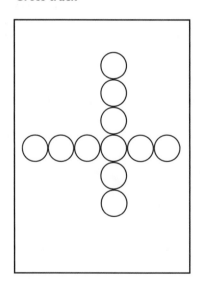

This shape is especially suitable for combinations of forward and sideways movements.
Step sequence: Forward: run (two ground contacts), sideways: sidesteps to the left or right, forward: two-footed bouncing jumps (2 ground contacts).

Hoop track with gaps

A hoop track can also be set up with a gap in it (about 5 yards wide), in which the players can carry out additional activities. The activities are similar to those for the railroad track. Two examples are shown below.

• *Step sequence*: Run: 2 ground contacts in each tire - run - 90-degree turn - touch the cone - 90-degree turn - jumps: open/close.

• *Step sequence*: Jumps: open/close - run - complete rotation - run: 2 ground contacts in each hoop

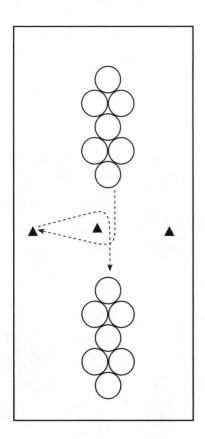

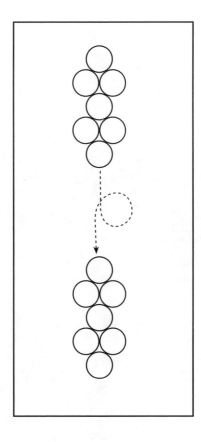

Row of hoops

If a row of hoops is set up, other movement drills can be carried out. Hopping and running movements can be combined with dummy steps. Dummy steps to the outside should finish with a tap step.

Step sequence: Two steps in the tire - dummy step to the right - tap - two steps - dummy step to the left - tap - and so on.

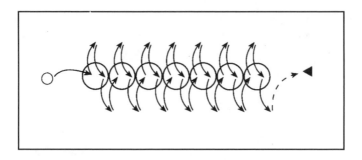

Row of hoops: cross steps (back - front)

Row of spaced hoops

Short fast steps should be made in the gaps between the hoops.

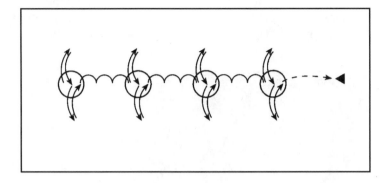

Circle of hoops

Fast foot and leg movements can be practiced very well in the circle of hoops. Six yellow hoops are arranged around a red hoop.
The players start from the center and move outward (to the side, forward, back) hoop by hoop in a given sequence.

Running and jumping drills

- Two-footed bouncing jumps
- One-footed bouncing jumps
- Fast running movements (two ground contacts)
- Cross steps

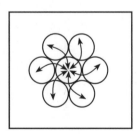

Row of hoops with diagonals

Rows of hoops made up of diagonal sequences of 3 to 5 hoops are very popular. They enable the players to carry out bouncing jumps, skips or fast foot movements with changes of direction. The range of variations is increased if the players hop forward over a number of hoops and then hop one hoop backward (e.g. 3 hoops forward and one backward).

Row of hoops with diagonals: bouncing jumps

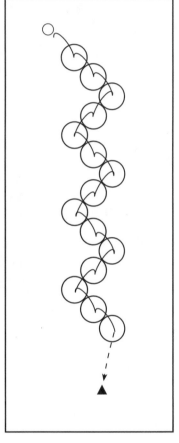

COMBINATION OF RODS AND HOOPS

Rods (hurdles) and hoops can be varied and combined in many different ways. For example, the players can start with drills involving rods and then finish with a Jumping Jacks hoop track. This arrangement teaches the players to respond to a number of demands in one drill.

Rods and hoops

The players should complete a hoop course, run and finish by carrying out the required activities on the railroad track.
The activities can be taken from the section "Railroad Track".

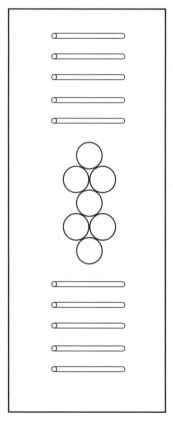

Rods and hoops

Hoops and rods

The players start with jumps along the hoop track and adjust quickly to running along the railroad track.

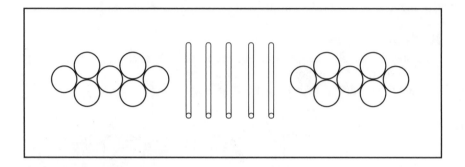

Alternating rods and hoops

Short hoop and rod phases require fast adjustment to the different movements demanded of the legs (jumps, step sequences, dummy steps), the whole body and, last but not least, the head.

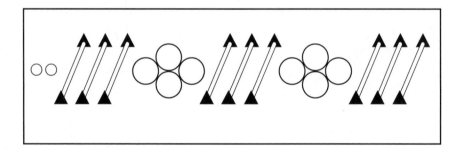

Two-footed bouncing jumps over hoops and rods

Jumps and dummy steps

Jumps over the hurdles are combined here with dummy steps in the hoops. After a player has jumped all the hurdles he hops into the first hoop, then out of it and then back into it. he does the same at the second hoop before jumping the next hurdle.

Jumps and dummy steps

Several hoops between successive rods

Three hoops between rods

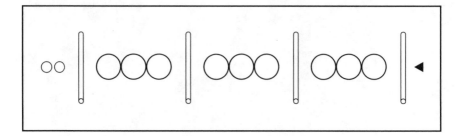

Four hoops between rods

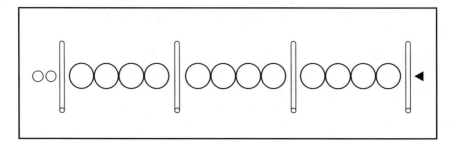

One-two arrangement of hoops between rods

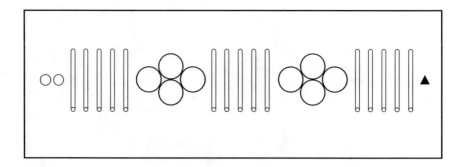

Increasing number of hoops between rods

The number of hoops between successive rods steadily increases, so the step sequence constantly changes (here: from two to five hoops).

Hoop and rod triangles, squares, pentagons, etc.

There are a large number of possible arrangements of hoops and rods.

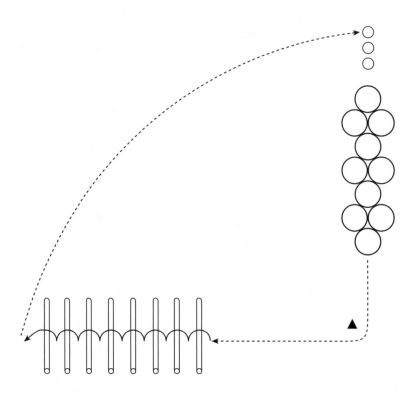

Hoop and rod triangle

Jumping Jack and sideways skips. The sequence starts with the hoop track, followed by a sprint around the corner cone and followed by sideways movements along the railroad track. The players then run back to their starting point.

Triangle of hoops and rods: Jumping Jack and skipping

Arm and leg coordination

The interaction of the large muscle groups (in this case arms and legs) plays a central role in general coordination conditioning. Many young players and adults find it difficult to control their arms and legs simultaneously, especially if the movements are not synchronous. They lose their rhythm because they concentrate on one part of the whole movement and thus carry out the other part incorrectly.

Skipping, Schuhplattler and Jumping Jack activities are excellent for coordinating arm and leg movements. The original Jumping Jack is familiar to most people, but there is such a wide range of variations of this activity, which makes considerable demands on coordination skills, that we have devoted a whole section to it.

SKIPPING

Jump ropes are accessories with which many coordination drills can be carried out, but their use in basic soccer coaching is steadily decreasing. However, every soccer club would do well to acquire 20 of them. Schoolteachers are in a better position, as jump ropes are part of the basic equipment of every school gymnasium.

Running and jumping
- Two hops per swing of the jump rope
- One hop per swing of the jump rope
- Running on the spot, raising the knees high
- Running in a space
- Kicking movements

SCHUHPLATTLER

Another interesting form of general coordination activity is the rhythmic lifting and touching of a foot, known as "schuhplattler." The sequence is: lift the foot, touch with the hand, place the foot on the ground again.

The foot can be touched with the hand on the same or the opposite side of the body, either in front of or behind the body. Important: bend the knee.

Schuhplattler without hops are less strenuous and easier to carry out. Schuhplattler with hops (each time a foot is raised, the player hops) make considerable demands on coordination and endurance. Some players have major problems in maintaining the given rhythm with both hands and feet, and considerable differences in the coordination of the movements are initially apparent.

Movements without hopping
- Front: left only
- Front: right only
- Front: left and right alternately
- Back: left only
- Back: right only
- Back: left and right alternately
- In turn: front right/left and back right/left

Movements with hopping
- Front right, hop
- Front left, hop
- Back right, hop
- Back left, hop

Combination with other movements
- Lifting the knee (compare "knee up" in the section "Soccerobics," page 120)
- Simple jumps
- Jumping Jack
- Combinations with ball

JUMPING JACK

The basic principle of the Jumping Jack and its variations is: opening and closing the legs, combined with various arm movements.

The movements should be rhythmical, possibly with background music. Experience with young players and adults shows that they can carry out the basic movements well, but have problems maintaining their rhythm when part of the movement changes. Coaching sessions in which the players combine arm and leg movements in a given rhythm help to improve the coordination skills of the players.

Important: The jumps and the opening and closing of the legs place considerable stress on the joints. Coaches should not overdo the Jumping Jack movements. After intensive practice sessions the players should carry out relaxation drills, light drills with the ball or stretching exercises.

To keep the stress on the joints as low as possible, the tips of the toes should point slightly outward and the knee should not be moved forward over the tips of the toes.

Normal Jumping Jack. This is the most familiar form of the Jumping Jack. The players stand with their legs closed and their arms at their sides. They then open their legs and pull their arms up over their head. They might clap their hands, although frequently the arms are simply lifted until they are just above the horizontal.

**Normal Jumping Jack: legs
closed, arms at sides (1)**

**Normal Jumping Jack: Legs open
and arms raised (2)**

Reverse Jumping Jack. The arms are at the player's sides when the legs are open, and they are lifted when the legs are together.

**Reverse Jumping Jack: legs
closed, arms raised (1)**

**Reverse Jumping Jack: Legs open
and arms at sides (2)**

Jumping Jack drills

The Jumping Jack can be varied in many ways to systematically increase the level of difficulty.

Jumping Jack with music	Various leg movements

Jumping Jack with ball	Various arm movements

Jumping Jack in hoop track	Various jumping rhythms

Jumping Jack on the move	Turns while carrying out the Jumping Jack sequence

- *Various leg movements:* The player can open his legs to the sides, diagonally or to front and back.
- *Various arm movements:* The arm movements can be varied in numerous ways to increase the level of difficulty
- *Various jumping rhythms:* The legs can be opened and closed quickly (open - shut) or slowly (open - hop, close - hop). In the slow version the players make a small intermediate hop, which puts no additional stress on the muscles.
- *Turns while carrying out the Jumping Jack sequence:* All Jumping Jacks turn through 90 degrees. The players should turn precisely. After 4 turns through 90 degrees they should be back in their starting positions. The players can turn as they open their legs or as they close them. These are two different activities, increasing the range of variation.

- *Jumping Jack on the move:* Forward and backward movements, possibly in combination with turns, introduce more variation and difficulty. Usually a Jumping Jack movement is carried out on the spot, but it can also be carried out on the move, making it more difficult. Possible movements:
  - forward-backward (important: constant forward jumping distance; smooth sequence of movements)
  - left and right (from cone to cone or line to line)
  - 90-degree turns
  - geometric forms (e.g. square/triangle)
- *Jumping Jack in hoop track:* The hoops define the distances for the jumps forward.
- *Jumping Jack with ball:* Jumping Jack movements with a ball are of special importance for soccer players. Bouncing, throwing and forward movements with a ball are combined with defined leg movements.
- *Jumping Jack with music:* Music helps the players to carry out the movements in harmony and creates a motivating "group feeling." The section on "Soccerobics" contains several ideas on this subject (page 108).

Arm movements. The arms can also carry out other movements. In the starting position the legs are closed and the arms have a defined initial position and sequence of movements. For example, an aerobic movement such as the butterfly could be carried out. It makes a difference whether the arms are moved forward or from front to back when they open. For the players this is a new drill.
- Arms parallel, forward - backward
- Rowing (arms backward - forward)
- Arms to the side, up to the horizontal position (limited swing)
- Arms parallel, upward - downward (starting position of arms: head/shoulder)
- Arms downward - upward
- Sparring - left and right alternately
- Butterfly movement
- Arms crossed

Butterfly: Arms closed (1)   **Butterfly: Arms open (2)**

Leg movements. The Jumping Jack can be made more difficult by additional leg movements. For example, after the legs are opened they can be crossed over as they close. A variation of the foot movements is to move the feet diagonally (once forward to the right - once forward to the left).

Crossed legs: Arms and legs open (1)

Crossed legs: Arms and legs crossed (2)

Crossed legs. There are two ways of crossing the legs. The simple way is to keep one foot at the front and the other at the back. Constantly changing the front foot when crossing the legs demands a higher level of coordination.

Crossed legs; as a variation
Sparring movements with the arms

Activities for advanced players. If players are asked to combine arm and leg movements, they will usually be able to do so without difficulty. The coach can make things more difficult by asking them to carry out two (or three or four) different activities in one drill.

- Keeping the arms parallel makes fewer demands on coordination than raising the stretched arms alternately or sparring with both arms. These arm movements disturb the stability of the movement as a whole. Beginners may lose their balance.
- Combinations of two different arm movements open up a wide range of variations. For example, opening and closing the legs can be accompanied by forward and backward or upward and downward arm movements. The advantage of combining two (rather than three) arm movements is that the first movement can be carried out as the legs are opened and the second as they are closed.

- Combining the opening and closing of the legs with three different arm movements is very difficult, as the body's movements constantly have to be varied. Players can only achieve this when the leg movements are automatic and they only have to concentrate on the arm movements. Concentrating on both arms and legs simultaneously is almost impossible. Example of sequence: Arms stretched to the side, then forward, then upward, etc.

Lift arms up and down while crossing legs

The arm movements remain the same but the legs are crossed instead of simply being closed. Initially this can be carried out with left or right always behind, but the ultimate objective is to change constantly. *Sequence:* Open - cross (left behind), open - cross (right behind), etc. The legs can be crossed in combination with a variety of arm movements. This increases the level of difficulty still further.

Arms stretched forward (1)

Arms alternately up and down (2)

Combinations. The combination of two (or more) leg movements creates more options for increasing the level of difficulty. For example, opening to the side and closing, repeated four times, can be combined with four forward and backward movements. The coach can give his creativity free rein.

Variation: Dummy step (forward-backward)
- right forward, together, right forward, etc.
- left forward, together, left forward, etc.
- ight forward, together, left forward, together, etc.

Jumping Jack and partner

Other possible variations, with lots of fun, are provided by the Jumping Jack as a drill for two players. An additional ball in the middle can be touched, transferred, thrown or bounced back and forth. Combinations with ball activities for each player (throwing up, catching, throwing to each other) also provide lots of options.

Jumping Jack with partner and ball: bouncing the ball to each other while opening the legs.

Speed and reaction

When we speak of a player's speed, we usually mean a combination of the following factors:
- Explosive starts, fast changes of direction, stops and turns
- Carrying out actions on the ball quickly
- Fast to react, size up game situations and act

According to Weineck (1998), the components of speed and their importance for a soccer player's performance are as follows.

Speed on the ball	Ability to run fast with the ball
Speed of movement	Ability to run fast
Speed of action	Fast and effective action, taking technical, tactical and conditional factors into account
Speed of reaction	Ability to react quickly to surprising game situations caused by teammates, opponents or the ball
Decision-making speed	Fast selection of the best and most effective solution in a given game situation
Speed of perception	Ability to perceive, process and evaluate the information appropriate to the game situation
Speed of anticipation	Anticipation of what teammates and opponents will do, based on experience and careful observation of the game

The drills in this section are intended to improve running technique, starting posture and the ability to change direction, which is very important for a soccer player. Sprinting ability and speed can also be improved by strength conditioning and reaction drills. Selective coordination conditioning, which builds up strength and the harmonious coordination of the muscles and groups of muscles involved in sprinting, results in a more explosive start and makes the players faster.

RUNNING TECHNIQUE

Many players have a poor running technique. They expend a lot of energy unnecessarily by moving the head, shoulders or torso, or fail to develop the necessary power for an explosive sprint because they do not stretch their ankles or knees fully. To eliminate these problems there are coordination exercises as well as drills and sprints with aids (rods, hurdles, etc.). Conditioning soccer players' running coordination mainly involves varying their stride length and frequency. This is done by varying the distances between and height of the hurdles, rods, etc.

- Small gap between hurdles - high stride frequency
- Large gap between hurdles - long stride length
- High hurdles - high knee lift

The coach should also focus on the development of strength (conditioning jumping strength) and agility (stretching exercises).

Main coaching elements

- Fast footwork
- Light-footed movements
- Changes of direction with sudden stops and acceleration
- Jumping strength conditioning
- Specified stride sequence, stride length and stride frequency

Running technique drills

Improving starting technique. Stretching the knees and ankles and using the arms properly can be checked with the "fall start." The player tenses his body and allows himself to fall forward (not bending at the hips) until he feels that he about to fall. Just before this happens, he starts his sprint.

Points to note

- Hands: Raise to chin height
- Angle at elbow: 90 degrees
- Take-off leg: fully stretched
- Knee: explosive knee action
- Thigh: raise to the horizontal

Improving the ankle action. The following drills can be used:
- Hurdling (stretch the whole body with emphasis on ankle action)
- Hopping with left/right (buildup: draw foot right up behind body)
- One-legged hopping over hurdles with an intermediate hop (flat)

SPRINTS

Sprints after initial activities

The players first carry out an activity, then they sprint.

A series of parallel rods lies on the ground, forming the start zone. When the players have run through this zone while carrying out an activity, they sprint for 10 yards. The rod zone can be made more demanding by using small hurdles (height up to 30 cm) instead of rods.

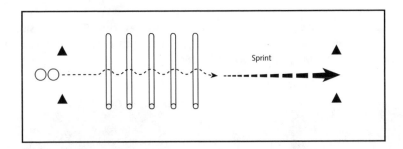

Activities
- Skip over the rods or hurdles
- Sprint over the rods or hurdles without touching them
- Skip or run sideways
- Hop on one foot (once on the left foot, then once on the right)
- Hop on two feet
- Skip two rods forward, one rod backward
- Delayed jumps with change of feet (distance greater)
- Skip sideways - two forward, one back

Jumping combinations or sideways skipping in the start zone. First the players carry out combinations of jumps or skip sideways over two parallel rods (from the middle to the left, back to the middle, to the right, to the middle, sprint), then they sprint over the other rods.

One against one. The sprint can also be started out of a 1 v 1 situation.

In the following drill both players jump so that they meet shoulder-to-shoulder, then they sprint to the cone.

Initial action   Sprint

Sprints with changes of direction, sudden stops and acceleration phases

Other forms of sprint conditioning involve changes of direction, sudden stops and acceleration phases.

Zigzag. Various activities can be carried out, such as the sprint-backward-sprint sequence. The players sprint from the first (yellow) to the second (red) cone, touch it and sprint backward, moving their feet quickly, until they can see the third (yellow) cone. Then they sprint to the fourth (red) cone, etc.

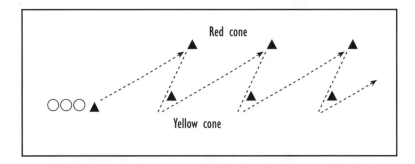

Touching the cone at the end of a sprint

Accelerating after the backward sprint

Variation: Now the players do not touch the first cone but sprint 2 feet past it, then back to the second cone, and then sprint forward.

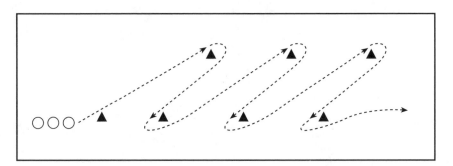

Forward - sideways - backward. The players sprint forward to the first cone, then sideways to the second and backward to the finishing cone. This drill should be carried out as fast as possible.

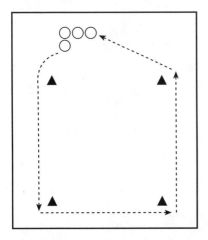

Dice five. The players sprint forward, sideways and backward in turn, with changes of direction and turns.

Sprint sequence: (1) Start from cone no. 1, (2) forward to the center cone no. 2, (3) turn through 90 degrees, sideways to the left to cone no. 3, (4) short sprint backward, (5) sideways to the center cone, (6) forward to cone no. 4, (7) rotate clockwise until facing final cone no. 5, sprint to the final cone.

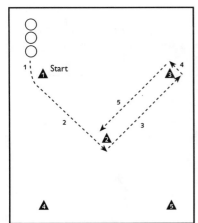
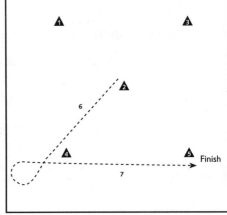

Sprint forward, then sidesteps to the left

Turn clockwise, then sprint forward to the finish

Drills for two players: Reacting in a square. Player A reacts to the sprint of player B and touches the appropriate cone. He either moves in parallel to his partner or mirrors his movements.

Partner dictates the sprint direction - parallel

Partner dictates the sprint direction - mirror image

Other organizational forms for sprinting

Sprints over hoops. The players carry out an activity in the hoop track - see p 40 - and then look at the coach (or their partner), who calls or signals that they should jump off the track. They then have to carry out another activity.

Activities (additional)
- a shot at goal after a short sprint
- a jumping or diving header (ball thrown)
- fast dribble through a slalom course

Sprints from a triangle of rods. During a game of soccer, sprints are often hindered by opponents or a change of direction of the ball. The players should thus be able to sprint powerfully and explosively even when they are hindered.

The players carry out a starting activity requiring full concentration, such as fast foot movements in a triangle formed by three rods. At a call or sign from the coach, they launch into a sprint. A cone placed 5 to 10 yards away from each triangle forms the turning or finishing point.

Sequence: The players run into the triangle, making two foot contacts with the ground, then run to the right, then back into the triangle, then left, then back into the triangle, then backward, etc.

Activities
- Two-footed bouncing jumps
- One-footed bouncing jumps (be careful: this puts a lot of stress on the ankles)
- Combination of hops and steps

Notes
- The rods can be placed on the ground or laid on small or large cones. Changing the height of the rods makes the players adjust their movements to the new demands.
- The speed of the activities should be appropriate to the level of ability of the players. Precision is more important than speed.
- Depending on the size of the group, 3 to 6 triangles should be set up.
- The activities in the triangles should be varied.

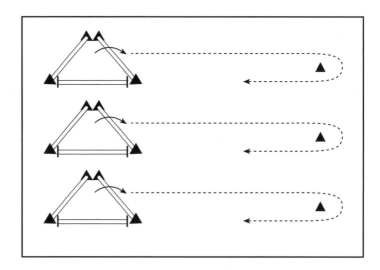

Variations
- On the way to the finish the players jump over additional small hurdles.
- Sprint with turn at the cone and short sprint back.
- To make the start more interesting, the coach can give different signals for stride sequences (arm up), hopping (arm to the side) and a starting activity (arm down).

Sprints out of a hoop circle. From the above configuration the start signal can also be given by a player who runs into space. Player A carries out fast foot movements in the hoop circle. Player B starts a run and calls for the ball, which is 2 to 5 yards in front of the hoop circle. Player A sprints to the ball and passes it into the path of player B.

Fast foot movements in the hoop circle

Sprint to the ball and pass

Variations
- A sprint to the ball, followed by a pass to the signaller, can also be carried out after various starting movements.
- The pass to the sprinting player is preceded by a challenge for the ball.

The start signal is the sprint by player A

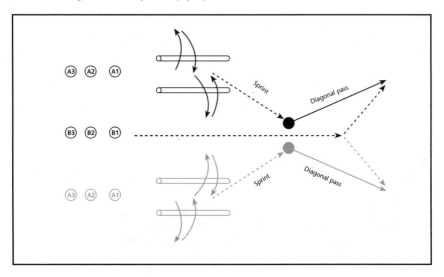

The start signal is the sprint to the ball

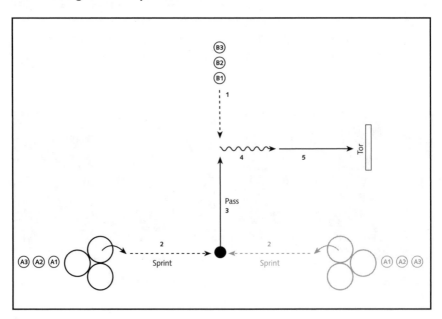

Sprints with additional activities in groups of three. The cones are 10 to 15 yards apart. Player A sprints toward player B, carries out an activity, turns and sprints toward player C, carries out the activity again, turns and sprints toward player B, and so on. If a ball goes wide of player B or C, they have to fetch it quickly so that the drill can be continued. It is advisable to place a second ball nearby.

Depending on the physical condition and age of the players, the drill should last for 30, 45 or 60 seconds.

Activities
- The passes from B and C must be passed back directly (one touch).
- The ball is thrown and headed back.
- The ball is thrown and volleyed back first time with the inside of the foot (activity for advanced players).

REACTION AND ORIENTATION

Number reaction run. Six cones numbered 1 to 6 are placed in a row between two lines. The players start in groups of three, four or five. The coach calls out a two-figure number composed of the numbers of the cones. The players sprint to the cones and touch those whose numbers were called out. A change of direction has to be made after the second cone has been touched. The finishing point of the sprint can therefore be behind cone 1 or behind cone 6.

Example 1: The coach calls out 25. The players sprint first to cone 2, touch it, and run (without changing direction) to cone 5. At cone 5 they change direction and run to the finishing cone (in this case, cone 1).

Example 2: The coach calls out 52. The players sprint first to cone 5, touch it, and run to cone 2 (change of direction). The players then change direction again and sprint to the finishing cone (cone 6).

Note: The cone numbers always remain the same. The players thus have to re-orientate themselves constantly. If they start the sprint at the first cone in the line the sequence of numbers is 1, 2, 3, 4, 5, 6. If they start at the last cone in the line, the sequence is 6, 5, 4, 3, 2, 1. This drill thus promotes the players' ability to concentrate while carrying out a movement.

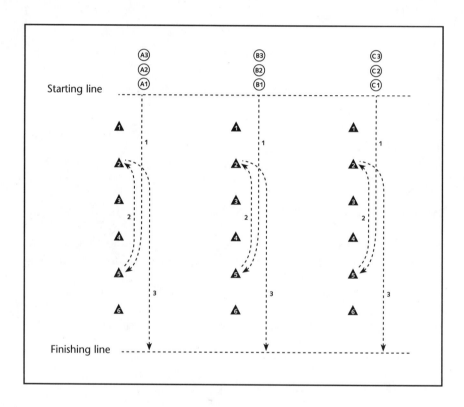

Games

Games are a lot of fun and are therefore especially suitable for young players.

Catch the hare. The rods are arranged in a circle like the rays of the sun. (Hoops or small hurdles can also be used.) Two players stand at opposite sides of the circle (hunter and hare). The hunter tries to catch the hare without touching the rods (hoops, hurdles).

Variation 1: The hunter runs as fast as he can in one direction (clockwise or counterclockwise). If the hare or the hunter touches a rod, he is the loser. If the hunter fails to touch the hare within a specified time (e.g., 30 seconds), the hare wins.

Variation 2: The hunter can change direction, so the hare cannot just put his head down and run but is forced to watch the hunter, otherwise he will simply run into his arms.

Catching the hare

Variations
- The coach can quickly vary the players' stride length by asking them to run closer to, or further away from, the middle.
- The coach or the hunter can specify the type of steps.
  - running, one ground contact between successive rods
  - running, two ground contacts between successive rods
  - sidesteps
  - bouncing jumps (one-footed/two-footed)

"Losing" an opponent. Two players are between two cones. Player A tries to "lose" player B by feinting and sidestepping. If he is able to touch the outside cone before player B touches the inside cone, he scores one point. Only when player A has sent his opponent the wrong way should he sprint to the cone. It is advisable to have a third player as a referee. The third player can also change places with one of the others at intervals.

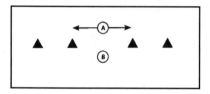

SPECIAL COORDINATION CONDITIONING

Basics

As soccer players gain in ability, the focus of coordination conditioning should shift from general to soccer-specific aspects. Soccer techniques should come to the fore while general coordination skills retreat into the background.

Demands made on a soccer player's coordination

Sport-specific coordination conditioning involves applying the movements that have been learned and doing so under conditions of varying degrees of difficulty. Soccer conditioning is about learning the necessary soccer techniques quickly and effectively. Coordination skills play an important role in this. Coordination must be learned in a soccer context so that the players can master the movement sequences and overcome the resistance factors of their sport.
• Jumping and then sprinting
• Changing direction rapidly after jumps, turns, resistance
• Movements in a restricted space
• Pressure from opponents
• Pressure of time
• Unusual weather conditions

Pressures on coordination

An attacker receives the ball and is challenged by a defender. He feels himself under a number of pressures. According to Neumaier (1999) these pressures can be summarized as follows.

Pressure of time
Demands deriving from the movement time or speed

Pressure of complexity
Simultaneous movements and/or sequential movements

Mental and physical pressure
Demands deriving from the physical and mental stress imposed by the conditions

Pressure to be accurate
Demands deriving from the need to move very precisely

Situational pressure
Demands deriving from the variability and complexity of the surroundings and the situation

Important:
Balance and awareness

Pressure of time. Modern soccer is so fast that there is a continuous requirement to act and move and to use soccer techniques at high speed. The players are therefore always under pressure of time. Experience and the ability to think ahead enable players to react faster and thus to reduce the pressure of time. Soccer reactions cannot, however, be planned in a straight line.

Mental and physical pressure. In a one-to-one situation a player is under considerable physical and mental pressure. The quality of coordination of his movements deteriorates when he is exhausted. Stress and fear can also put a lot of pressure on the player and crucially affect his movements. For example, in a one-to-one situation a player might be frightened to lose the ball and to disadvantage his team by passing the ball too late. This puts him in a stress situation, in which his otherwise good awareness and physical control are impaired.

Situational pressure. A player must not only control the ball but also observe the movements of his teammates and opponents. When a player receives a pass, the other players move toward the ball or take up good tactical positions (to be able to receive a pass or close down the available space). This means that the game situation is continuously changing and the players must continuously adjust to it.

The player receives a flood of information which he has to register and assess. In this complex and variable situation, the player has to be able to find the response with the best possible prospects of success (e.g. a dribble or a pass to a teammate).

Pressure to be accurate. Controlling and moving with the ball in a restricted space, well practiced feints and accurate crosses after beating an opponent require carefully judged use of energy.

Pressure of complexity. Numerous muscles are involved when a player challenges for the ball. They have to be used selectively and precisely, irrespective of whether the ball is on the right or left or an opponent challenges from the front or the side. Many movements proceed simultaneously, e.g. controlling the ball while looking around to size up the situation and shielding the ball from an opponent.

The demands made on a player's coordination are also increased as movements follow each other in sequence, e.g. controlling and running with the ball, feinting, dribbling at speed and crossing accurately.

In special coordination drills the players learn how to cope with these pressures. Such pressures should not affect their soccer technique or cause them to make the wrong decision in a complex game situation.

Technique and coordination conditioning

The boundaries between technique and coordination conditioning are fluid and, in fact, overlap. "The execution of a movement involves all aspects of coordination that are also necessary for good performance. It is therefore wrong to ask whether movement conditioning is (specific) technique conditioning or general conditioning. In fact we should ask what proportion of the drills is specific and what proportion is general." (Neumaier 1999).

Coordination or technique conditioning

Technique conditioning *(skill conditioning)*	Coordination conditioning *(ability conditioning)*

Setting targets *of the coaching situation (coaching targets/coaching content)* **Weighting** *of soccer-specific and general proportions*

Coordination-oriented **Technique Conditioning** • Technique application drills *(variable technique conditioning)* • Technique variation conditioning	*Technique-oriented* **Coordination Conditioning** • Specific coordination conditioning • Variation of the pressure conditions

Technique-oriented coordination conditioning

General coordination conditioning drills can be combined with the techniques of a given type of sport. Handball players can vary typical handball sequences, hockey players can use a hockey stick and soccer players should practice carrying out soccer-specific movements involving overcoming a degree of resistance (e.g. hurdles or hoops). This section combines general coordination drills with soccer-related finishing activities. In short, technique-oriented coordination conditioning in soccer means coordination conditioning plus ball drills.

Drills for 2 players

Player A carries out the drill while player B acts as the passer.

Jumping plus technical activity. Player A jumps over a rod and immediately carries out a technical activity with the ball played or thrown to him by player B.

Activities (technique)
- Low pass (with/without controlling the ball)
- Hip-high pass (with/without controlling the ball)
- Side-foot the ball hip-high back to the thrower
- Header from a standing position or after a jump and turn
- Play back the thrown ball

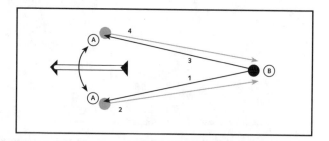

Jump over rod

Technical activity: Side-foot the hip-high ball back to the thrower

Pair of rods and technical activity. Fast foot movements and jumps before using soccer techniques promote the player's flexibility in game situations where unpredictable events occur. The activities on the track and the technical activity should be varied as much as possible.

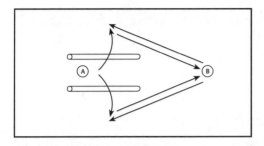

Two pairs of parallel rods: two-foot-ed bouncing jumps

Technical activity: header

Rod or hurdle and technique. Two or one-footed bouncing jumps over a rod or hurdle are especially suitable for combining with various activities for practicing technique.

Note: The coach should pay close attention to the execution of the two-footed bouncing jump, so that the players learn to adopt the ideal body position for the required technique on both right and left.

Activities (technique)
- Low pass (with/without controlling the ball)
- Hip-high pass (with/without controlling the ball)
- Header from a standing position or after a jump and turn
- Diving header

Returning a hip-high ball   **Important: use both feet**

Hoop track and finishing activity. A hoop course can also be the starting point.

Hoop track: Jumping Jack   **Finishing action: Pass on the turn**

Group drills

The application of soccer technique when a player is faced with obstacles can also be practiced in small groups (3 or 4 players) as a continuous drill or with the whole team as a large-group drill.

Heading drills in groups of three. Player A stands in the goal with a ball in his hand. Two players are on a track made from rods and hoops. Player A throws the ball to player B who heads it at goal while on the run (jumping or diving header). Players A and B then swap roles. B now throws the ball to player C, and so on.

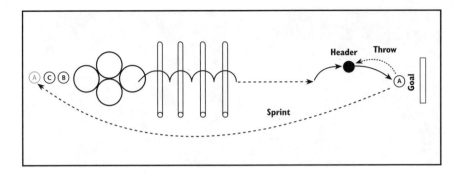

One-two in group of four. A threads his path through the rods, runs toward the goal and receives a pass from B. A plays a one-two with B and shoots at goal. A then takes the position of goalkeeper C, who takes the position of player B, who runs to the start position. It is advisable to have 2 players at the position initially occupied by B, so that no unnecessary delays occur.

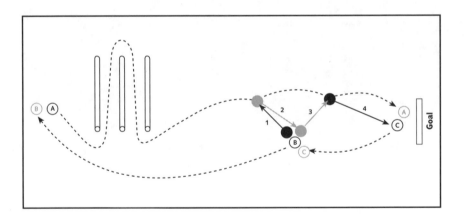

Group drill in continuous circuit. A variety of activities in association with running with the ball can be organized as follows for the whole team in a continuous circuit.

Two groups are assigned different tasks. The players in group A act as servers, while the players in group B carry out activities over a series of rods, return a pass/throw to the server and run to the next part of the circuit. The activities can be varied (sidesteps, cross steps, bouncing jumps, slalom, etc.) or just one activity can be chosen for the sake of simplicity. The distances between the rods or hoops depend on the size of the group. The servers should alternately throw the ball and play it low so that the players constantly have to adjust their technique. On one occasion a low return pass to the server is needed, then a header or a hip-high side-footed pass. The servers must take the level of skill of the receivers into account.

After a given time (10 to 15 minutes) the groups exchange positions. Group A goes to the start while the group B players go to the serving positions.

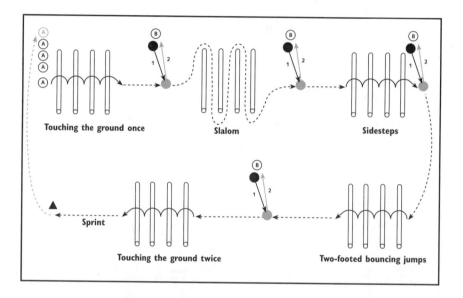

Variation: Goals can also be incorporated. They should always be occupied by two goalkeepers, so that the players do not have to wait if they shoot wide of the goal. In this case a reserve ball comes into use and the second goalkeeper fetches the ball that went wide.

Complex drills

Fast passes and coordination drills. The players are under pressure of time when they have to make first-time passes between two cones and then run around a circuit. The circuit should be designed to give the players a good chance of arriving at the starting point before the last player starts his run, so that the sequence of passes is not interrupted. The coach must also ensure that the activities are not too easy and the players are always under pressure of time. The coach can give his imagination free rein in designing the circuit.

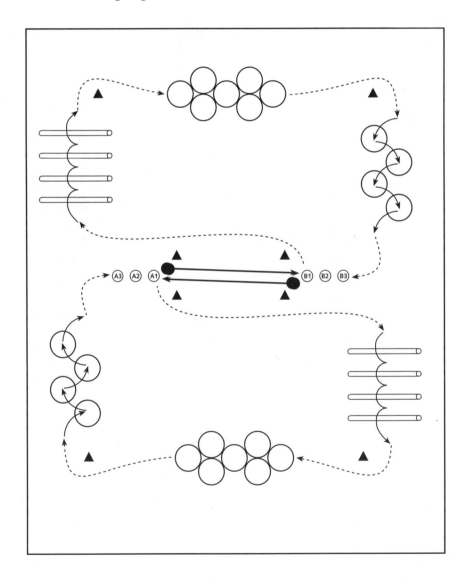

Complex drill. Two goals (one fixed goal, one mobile goal) are 30 to 40 yards apart. If no mobile goal is available, rods or cones can be used. Two sequences of rods or hoops are created 16 to 20 yards apart. Between them is a cross, formed by four rods.

Two players start simultaneously at opposite ends and have to adjust their speed to each other after crossing the sequence of rods or hoops. After running through the cross (90 or 270 degrees) they carry out an activity in front of the goal (e.g. pass, header, shot) and join the opposite group. If they have to score a goal, a goalkeeper should be in the goal. If they have to pass, the runner swaps positions with the player in the goal.

Activities (course)
- Running forward, touching the ground twice between successive rods or hoops
- Bouncing jumps (two-footed or one-footed)
- Running backward, touching the ground twice between successive rods or hoops
- Skipping sideways

Two players run through the cross simultaneously

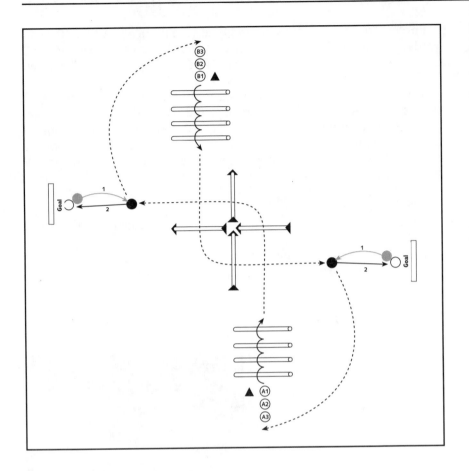

Variations

- *Middle:* The players run through or jump over the cross (90 or 270 degrees) and sprint toward the goal.
- *Goal:* Skilled players can carry out activities involving difficult techniques in front of goal, such as a first-time hip-high volley or a diving header. Spare balls should be available to avoid delays.

Coordination-oriented technique conditioning

Technique conditioning in a variety of situations (using technique in practice, variation drills) improves soccer-related coordination to a high degree. The drills are mainly focused on balance and ball control when passing, receiving the ball, running with the ball and heading.

BALANCE AND BODY CONTROL

A soccer player needs to be able to find his balance again quickly after jumping, turning and confrontations with opponents (shoulder charges, pushes, shirt pulling, etc.). Static and dynamic balance are important in the game of soccer. The success of an attacking run with the ball, for example, may depend on maintaining good body posture and a good position relative to the ball.

This is clear when a player follows up a jump or a turn with a shot at goal. He has to get his body into the right position for the shot as quickly as possible. At the same time he may have to overcome the challenge of an opponent and immediately recover his balance. A skilled opponent can use his body to unbalance a player just as he receives a pass. The opponent's task is to prevent the player from controlling the ball undisturbed. An experienced player can deal with this and recover quickly.

Players should experience such challenges on the training pitch, in combination with various techniques that will help to overcome them. Experienced players can cope with challenges without losing their balance.

The following additional drills are helpful:
- Drills on one leg
- Turns and jumps followed by an activity requiring the application of a technique

CHALLENGES

During coordination-related technique conditioning, techniques are practiced in situations where challenges have to be overcome (pulls and pushes). Players have to learn to continuously adjust their posture to maintain their balance. The players who are challenging must be aware that although their actions are allowed for the purpose of these drills, pushes and pulls will be punished by the referee under normal circumstances.

Challenge when receiving the ball   **Challenge when passing**

Hopping on one leg while handling a ball. Group drills with a ball can be carried out on one leg. The players have to disrupt their opponents' rhythm without losing their own ball.

Hopping on one leg and throwing a ball into the air.

BALL CONTROL

Juggling. All types of juggling drills improve a soccer player's ball control. Time is needed before beginners can juggle with a ball and develop good ball control. The following learning stages have proved useful.

Stage 1: Throw the ball a short distance into the air, play it back into the air once and catch it (foot, thigh, head) so that the player can use his muscular system under simplified conditions.

Stage 2: Combination of two parts of the body: throw the ball into the air, foot, thigh, catch - throw the ball into the air, thigh, foot, catch.

Stage 3: Throwing the ball higher into the air makes everything more difficult.

Stage 4: Juggle with the ball for as long as possible. Initially it does not matter if the ball falls to the ground occasionally.

Stage 5: More concentration is needed if the ball is regularly allowed to bounce once between juggling movements.

Stage 6: Experienced players juggle the ball without allowing it to bounce.

Variation: Juggling can also be practiced in groups of two or more. A player controls the ball, juggles it for a while and plays it to another player. The ball can also be played first time without a control touch.

Drills with additional activities

When a player carries out an activity with a ball (juggling, dribbling, passing, technique drills, etc.) he can concentrate on it. This is more difficult if a second activity, a second or third ball or another player is introduced.

Dribbling with two balls. The application of a technique is made more difficult by introducing a second ball.

A player dribbles not with one ball but with two. He should gradually increase the speed with which he dribbles the two balls, so that he has to concentrate more and more.

Variations
• The two balls can be of different size and weight.
• Skilled players can dribble three balls.

Dribbling with two balls

Moving forward with ball at feet while catching another ball. A player moves forward with one ball at his feet while he regularly throws a second ball into the air and catches it.

Moving forward with ball at feet while catching another ball

Moving forward with ball at feet while bouncing another ball. A player moves forward with one ball at his feet while he regularly bounces a second ball. The degree of difficulty can be increased by dribbling around a course or bouncing the ball with one hand and then the other. The activities with hands and feet should be varied so that the player faces new challenges, thus conditioning his coordination.

Moving forward with ball at feet while bouncing another ball

Bouncing the ball with the feet. The player bounces the ball with the sole of one foot then the other.

Bouncing the ball with the foot

Bouncing the ball with the foot and throwing another ball into the air

Variation. Having to concentrate on an additional activity makes the basic task more difficult. While the player bounces the ball with the feet he throws a ball into the air and catches it again.

Notes
- Initially the players should practice the technique of bouncing the ball with the sole of the foot until they have mastered it.
- Skilled players can bounce or throw one ball into the air with one hand and another with a foot.

Throwing one ball into the air and throwing another to a second player. This drill is suitable not just for goalkeepers but for all field players. A creative coach can vary and extend the drill.

Each of the two players must throw a ball into the air while they both throw a third ball back and forth to each other. They must use their right and left hands.

Player on the left: Throw one ball into the air with the left hand and another to the second player with the right hand.

Player on the right: Throw one ball into the air with the right hand at the correct moment and wait for the other ball and catch it with the left hand.

Two players and two balls. Player A holds a ball in both hands. Player B passes the ball along the ground to player A. As player B passes, player A throws his ball into the air, then he passes player B's ball back to him and catches his own ball again.

If the players are standing the correct distance apart and have found the correct passing speed and throwing height, they can carry out this drill precisely several times in succession.

Player on the left: Throw ball into the air, pass ball back to partner, catch ball again

Player on the right: Throw ball into the air, head ball back to partner, catch ball again

Variations
- The pass along the ground can be replaced by a throw and a header back. This looks easier than it is. The players should not concentrate too hard on throwing the ball into the air and catching it, otherwise they will not be able to head the other ball properly.
- Instead of throwing a ball into the air, the player could bounce or juggle an additional ball. The ball should then bounce up once without any contact by the player and immediately be involved again.
- This drill illustrates the principle of making a mastered technique more difficult with the help of an additional ball or activity.

Drills with different balls in groups of two or more

Drills should be carried out with different balls to help the players learn how to weight their passes. These drills teach the players to adjust to changes in the ball's weight, size, height of bounce, etc. The effect is enhanced because the ball control techniques continuously change.

Different balls: for volleyball, soccer, gymnastics, handball and mini soccer

Activities (different balls)
- Heading
- Passing: low
- Passing: volley with inside of foot
- Hip-high volleys on the turn
- Control with the chest before passing

Passing different balls. Each player has a stock of different balls (large and small soccer balls, water balls, tennis balls, softballs, etc.). Using various techniques, the balls are passed or thrown to a partner, who has to continuously adjust to balls of different weights and sizes. After the receiver controls the ball a new one is chosen.

Activities (server)
- Throw
- Pass along the ground
- Throw ball up and pass it

Activities (receiver)
- Inside of foot
- Instep
- Chest
- Thigh

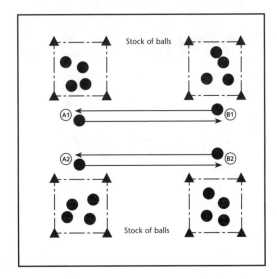

Variation: Group of four: Another player can carry out an activity prior to the pass or after the receiver controls the pass. This player then chooses a different ball.

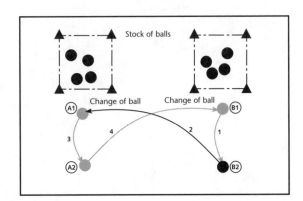

Controlling a tennis ball

Header with a volleyball

Passing in a group of three. In a group of three, player A throws a softball and player B throws a soccer ball to player C, who plays the balls back first time in succession (head or foot).

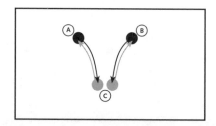

Volleyed shot after thrown pass

Variations
- The three players position themselves so that player C has to turn through 90 degrees to receive the ball and play it back (here: the thrown ball is being headed back to the thrower). The players vary the height and target of the throws and passes.
- Different balls can also be used for this drill.

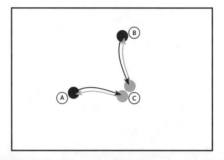

Fast turn before heading the ball

Change of serve. Player A plays the ball low and receives a low return pass from player C. Player B throws the ball high and player C heads the ball back to him.

Note: To ensure that the drill flows smoothly, the second player should throw the ball. Skilled players can also accurately volley the thrown ball back to the thrower.

Activities
- Using different balls
- Diving header
- Hip-high volley on the turn

Pass along the ground with turn through 180 degrees

Header after turning around

Servers stand at different distances. The drill can be varied with different targets. Player A stands 5 yards from player C, while player B stands 15 to 20 yards from player C. Player C now has to play the balls back accurately at an appropriate pace to players A and B.

Variation: The servers can vary their positions so that the receiver continuously has to reorientate himself.

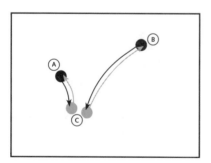

Weighted passing game. This drill mainly improves the players' ability to pass the ball into space, which is an essential part of opening up a defense. The ball should not be played too short or too fast.

The drill is carried out over a series of parallel rods with a subsequent dribbling activity. The player passes the ball forward and then sprints over the rods. His objective is to reach the ball before the first cone and then make several changes of direction or turns with the ball.

The distance to the first cone depends on the age and ability of the players. It is essential to change the distance frequently, so that the players have to constantly adjust the pace of the forward pass.

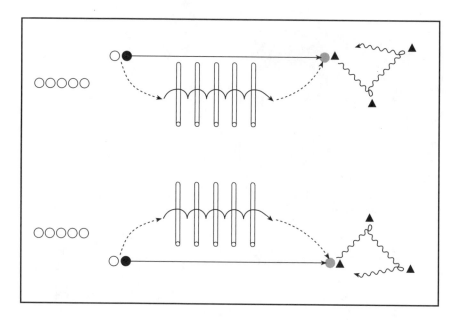

Forward pass followed by sprint over low hurdles (1)

Watch the ball and run quickly over the rods (2)

After reaching the ball, dribble with changes of direction

NEED TO ACT QUICKLY

In modern soccer, players have to act quickly. They rarely have the time to look calmly at the ball and the game situation before they decide what to do. The higher the pace of the game, the better the players should be conditioned to deal with it. They must practice the necessary soccer-specific techniques under variable conditions and especially under pressure of time.

The stress and the need to act quickly that are encountered in an important game with determined opponents are difficult to simulate. Nevertheless, coaches can combine the use of soccer techniques with a time factor. Relay competitions, pursuit races or group competitions incorporating various techniques can be used to make players think more about the time factor than their technique. If this is done variably and the players are well motivated, this will prepare them to handle the pressure in match situations when they have to act quickly. Another way to simulate such situations is to time the players as they use various techniques.

Group competitions

Group competitions have one big advantage - they are a lot of fun. Technique conditioning is not central but is certainly an integral aspect. The group pressure causes the players to concentrate and this simulates the stress situations of a real game. A number of group competitions are described on the following pages.

Dribblers versus jugglers. The faster the players dribble round a cone, the fewer ball contacts the players in the other group have.

One or more players in group B juggle a ball and a referee counts the number of ball contacts. The players of group A dribble as fast as they can around a marked area (square, rectangle). When all of the players of group A have reached the finishing point the referee stops counting the number of ball contacts of group B. After the dribblers have made three runs the two teams swap places. The dribblers become jugglers and vice versa. The juggling team with the most ball contacts wins.

Note: One member of the juggling team (or more, if more counters are present) plays the ball into the air with a foot, a knee or his head. Each ball contact counts. The ball can touch the ground but must not be picked up with the hand.

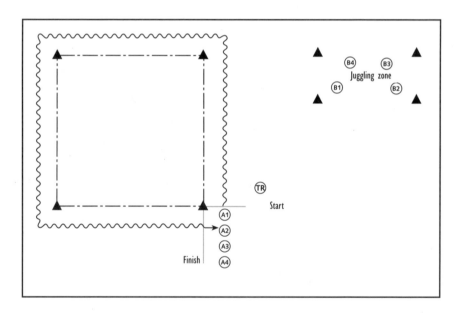

Variations
- In the "easy" version the players simply run with the ball around the marked area, thus fixing the time available to the jugglers.
- The dribblers have a more difficult task if they have to carry out additional activities on their way to the finish (slalom around cones, passes against a wall, jump over a hurdle, etc.)
- The activities carried out by group B can be changed. Options include drop-kicks against a wall or headers or shots into a goal.

Dribbling versus one-touch play. The competitive principle of group A against group B with various activities can also give the following competition.

Group A dribbles around a defined course and group B plays a ball back and forth between two cones. The dribblers define the time, because when all of the dribblers have reached the finish the referee stops counting the passes.

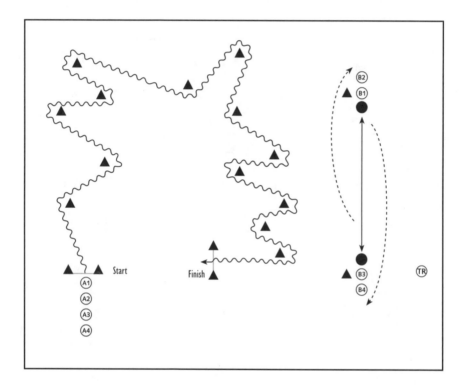

One against one competitions

Pursuit race. Cones are set up to form a slalom course. The idea is to dribble a ball through the cones as fast as possible. Player A sets off first, followed by player B. Player B wins if he catches player A before player A reaches the finish. After one run the players swap roles.

The coach decides how much of a start to give player A. Player B must have a realistic chance of catching him. If player A loses control of the ball or misses a cone, this counts as being caught.

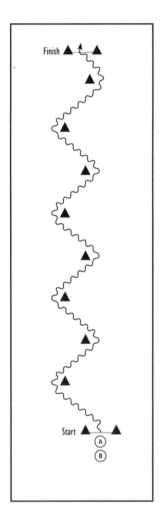

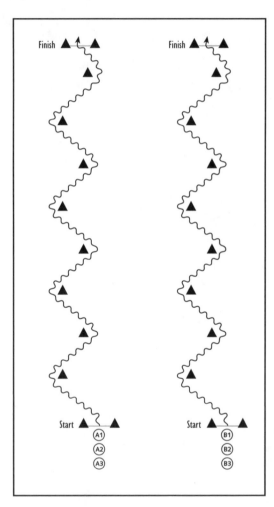

Double course. This form of competition is very popular with young players. If the activities are chosen well, older players also enjoy it.

This can be similar to the catcher race if the players compete against each other on two equal courses. The winner is immediately apparent. If there is a dead heat a decider is held.

Timed dribbling and shooting course. Timed competitions are easy to organize. The players' times can be used to create a ranking list and this motivates the players to do their best. However, the organization of these competitions should not be too complex.

The players might be divided into three groups. Two teams play 5 against 5 and the third team goes around the course. Then it is the turn of the next group, etc.

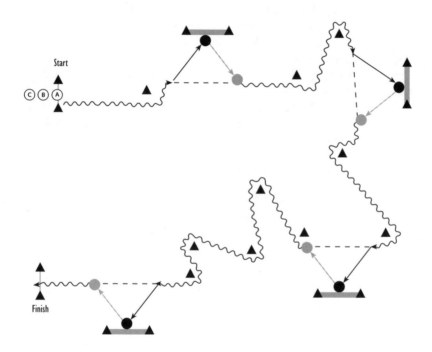

SOCCEROBICS - COORDINATION CONDITIONING WITH BALL AND MUSIC

Basics

Soccerobics is coordination conditioning with a ball, combining aerobic elements with soccer-typical movements. It improves coordination skills (e.g. coordination of arms and legs), endurance, strength (especially the leg muscles) and muscular endurance as well as agility.

Elegant and fluid ball control and the ability to move economically and esthetically have their origins mainly in childhood. The development of a good sense of rhythm and ball skills makes the difference between soccer as play and soccer as work. This means that children should develop and improve a feeling for rhythm and movement as early as possible in the context of conditioning exercises.

- *Soccerobics* uses the fascination of music and combines it with soccer techniques and exercises to develop important aspects of conditioning that are of major significance for soccer players.
- *Soccerobics* is thus not only a method of improving coordination skills but is also eminently suitable for conditioning at all levels of age and performance.

A Soccerobics group

Notes

Initially the players learn to listen to the rhythm of the music and translate it into movement.

Exercises that involve touching or moving a ball are of key importance for soccer players. Initially these are simple foot and leg movements, touching the ball but without hopping. When the players are familiar with these movements, arm and ball movements can be introduced. This promotes arm and leg coordination.

The program of exercises is suitable for all players of all ball games and develops their coordination skills.

Soccerobics can be practiced in many situations

- Soccerobics is suitable for warming up as well as for energetic conditioning drills. Their main purpose is conditioning. Depending on what the coach wants to achieve, the drills can be carried out at a lower (stepping movements) or higher intensity (hopping movements).
- Soccerobics exercises can be carried out individually, in pairs or in groups.
- Soccerobics can be carried out indoors or outdoors.
- Music is not absolutely essential, but helps to motivate the players. The music should support the movements (energetic movements = fast music) and be aligned to the participants' interests.

Rhythm

The rhythm of sports movements dominates and is defined by the coach's counting. If a coach does not have the confidence to support the changing movements by counting, he should ask the players to concentrate on their rhythm themselves.

Concentration

Strict sequences of movements with programmed changes promote concentration under pressure of time; they are aligned to the music and the coach's counting. Skilled players can carry out fast changes of arm and leg movements. These activities are very demanding and require practice. Wide differences in ability may become apparent within a group. In the course of time the players learn to concentrate on the coach's instructions, although the level of physical exertion is sometimes very high and they must overcome their own internal resistance.

Coordination of arms and legs

At the International Coaches Congress of the Federation of German Soccer Instructors (BDFL) in Schmallenberg in 1999 the junior players of Bayer Leverkusen demonstrated a drill with two balls. They kicked one ball back and forth while simultaneously throwing a second one. From a distance this looked very easy. However, everyone soon realized that a very high level of coordination was required. Two trainee coaches attempted to repeat the drill and it was immediately clear that they had considerable problems coordinating their foot and arm movements. They lost their rhythm and usually simple movements such as shooting and throwing became very inaccurate.

Ball on the ground

Soccer players often have to adjust their posture and position to a rapidly changing game situation. To do this they have to be able to make fast foot and leg movements and they need excellent body control. In addition, players need to be able to quickly adjust the rhythm of their runs to new situations. The following exercises combine soccer movements with a musical rhythm.

Moving the ball

Initially the players tap the ball back and forth in all directions across a 15 x 15 yard square to a musical accompaniment so that they can try out the activities specified by the coach. The taps can be accompanied by paces or hops. Hopping is more strenuous.

Activities (feet)
- Tap the ball forward/backward with the tip of the foot
- Tap the ball to left and right in turn across the standing leg
- Turns around the ball
- Move the ball in a circle (clockwise and counterclockwise)

Arm movements

As the players tap the ball they can make arm movements (or even tap a second ball). This conditions the arms and legs and warms up the upper body. This is especially suitable for the start of a coaching or Soccerobics session.

Rowing: forward - backward

Rowing: upward

**Butterfly: elbows at shoulder
height, bring the arms together in front of the head (1)**

Open arms outward (2)

Other arm movements

- Draw up both shoulders or move them in a circle (forward/backward)
- Move both arms in a circle
- Bend the arms outward in front of the body, parallel to the ground (biceps curl)
- Stretch the arms in front of the body and move them apart (expander)
- Box with both arms in turn; parallel forward, parallel downward, crossed in front, parallel downward
- Stretch the arms backward (triceps curl)
- Raise the stretched arms from the thighs above the head

Moving the arms in a circle. Taps and arm circling are difficult for beginners, who may easily lose their rhythm. Initially the arms can be held out in front of the body, parallel to the ground, and moved in a circle. When the players carry out large circling movements (swimming the crawl, or lifting the arms above the head) they must be able to tap the ball automatically so that they can concentrate on their arm movements.

Stretching the arms backward (triceps curl)

Triceps curl: arms bent (1)

Triceps curl: stretch the arms backward (2)

Raising the stretched arms from the thighs above the head (1)

Raising the stretched arms from the thighs above the head (2)

Tapping the ball on the spot (ball in front of player)

After tapping the ball back and forth across a marked area to familiarize themselves, the players take up their positions so that the coach can give targeted instructions.

A distinction is made between tap steps (right and left in turn), tap hops (right and left in turn) and combinations of both. The tap movements can be carried out backward (tap - back), to the side, away from the standing leg (tap - outside) or toward the standing leg (tap - inside). These soccer-relevant movements can also be combined. Then the coach counts: tap - outside, tap - inside.

Tap-back

Place the tip of the foot on the ball

Quickly pull the foot back

Tap - outside

Place the foot briefly on the ball

Quickly move the foot to the side

Tap - inside

 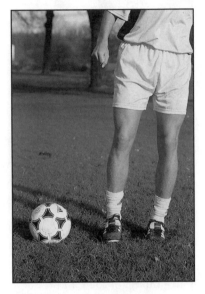

**Touch the ball by moving the foot
to the side**

**Quickly pull the foot back
toward the standing leg**

Combinations
- Tap - back, tap - outside
- Tap - back, tap - inside
- Tap - back, tap - outside, tap- inside
- Tap - pull the to the left / right
- Double tap: right - right, left - left (very strenuous)
- Single - single - double (right, left, right - right, left, right, left - left ...)
- Additional arm movements (with and without a ball)
- Drills for groups of two with a third ball: Player A and player B face
  each other and make an additional movement with a ball, which they
  touch, throw to each other or bounce to each other

Ball between the feet. The ball is on the ground between the feet. The players touch the ball with the tip of the left and right foot in turn, using a step or hop movement.

Ball between feet (1)

Tap with right foot, then return foot to ground (2) and (3)

Tap with the left foot (4)

Variation: Additional arm movement (with or without a second ball; see p 112 and p 113).

Drills for groups of two with a third ball. Two players face each other and start tap movements simultaneously. In addition they throw or bounce a third ball back and forth.

Ball in the hand

With a ball in the hand there are a large number of possible variations for arm movements while the legs carry out all kinds of step and hop movements. The emphasis is on coordination.

Movement drills

All participants carry a ball. At a signal from the coach they start to move back and forth across the marked area in time to the music. After a short familiarization period, arm movements are incorporated.

This is a relaxation drill after strenuous tap and hop movements. Because both arm and foot movements are carried out, this promotes the coordination of arms and legs. The more difficult the arm movements, the more easily the players lose their rhythm.

Activities (ball in hand)
- Squeeze the ball (with both hands, in front of the abdomen)
- Ball forward / backward
- Ball up / down (also diagonal to left / right)
- Throw the ball in the air and catch it (with or without clapping the hands)
- Biceps curl with the ball
- Move the ball in a circle (horizontal / vertical; / around the body)
- Bounce the ball (both hands / right / left hand)
- Combinations of the above activities

Jogging and throwing the ball in the air and catching it

Jogging and bouncing the ball with both hands

Practicing outdoors in a formation

All drills that involve hopping are strenuous. The coach should continuously vary jumping and relaxation drills to ensure that the ankles and knees are not overtaxed.

Knee-up, lift the ball

Knee-up (without intermediate hops). The players raise the left and right knees in turn in time to the music. As soon as the foot touches the ground again, the player raises the other knee. No pauses are allowed.

* Knee-up without ball (familiarization with the movement)
* Knee-up, move ball with both hands:
  * ball to the side of the thigh
  * ball forward - backward
  * ball diagonally high - back
  * ball up - down
* Knee-up and throw and catch (8 to 12 inches)
  * throw the ball two-handed in the air
  * throw the ball from one hand to the other
  * throw the ball up, clap hands, catch it again
* Knee-up and move ball to thigh
  * Arms forward
  * Raise arms with ball

- Knee-up and propel the ball into the air with the thigh
  - straight up (4 to 12 inches)
  - diagonally to the side

Move ball to thigh

Propel ball into air

Propel ball diagonally to the side

Kicking movements

Activities (legs)
- Jogging on the spot
- Jogging forward/backward in formation
- Jogging diagonally forward/backward
- Jogging and turning
- Hopping on both feet
- Kicking movements
- Twisting
- Leg curl
- Squat

Twisting

Leg curl

Activities (arms with ball against inside of foot)
- Arms forward
- Raise arms with ball

Squat

Ball against inside of foot

Activities (ball against instep)
- Arms forward
- Raise arms with ball
- Kick ball back into hands from instep

Ball against instep

Knee lift (with hop). In contrast to the knee-up, the players make a small hop as they change feet. This may be difficult for beginners at first, but they are soon able to carry out the movement in time with the music. The physical effort involved should not be underestimated. Strenuous drills should therefore alternate with less strenuous ones.

Important: After very strenuous phases the players should carry out stretching exercises for the muscles at the front and back of the lower legs.

Knee lift with ball held above the head

Jack 1 with various ball movements. When fast Jumping Jack movements (opening and closing the legs) are made without an intermediate hop, this is termed a Jack 1.

Activities (ball)
- Down, up
- Up, down
- Forward, back
- Throw, catch (no higher than head height)

Jack 1 with double ball movements

- Down, down - up, up
- Forward, forward - back, back
- Up, up - down, down
- Bounce, bounce - hold the ball when closing the legs

Combinations. The two drills described above can be combined in various ways. The level of difficulty can be increased if a regular sequence has to be carried out, such as the following combination.

Sequence: Four knee lifts forward, four Jumping Jacks on the spot - four knee lifts backward - four Jumping Jacks on the spot. If different arm or ball movements are incorporated, there are numerous opportunities for formulating a variable Soccerobics program.

Combinations in a limited space. Variations in a limited space can increase the complexity of the drill.

- Practice on the spot
- Practice with turns on the spot
- Practice in formation forward and backward
- Practice diagonally forward and backward (to left and right)

Drills in groups of two or more

Drills in groups of two are important as well as being very popular with young players. Applying the movements they have learned together with a partner is fun and stimulates creativity.

Two players stand around 2 yards apart and try to carry out a given movement synchronously. The start signal can be given by the coach or one of the players.

Drills to music in groups of two

Activities (legs)
- Jogging
- Hopping
- Knee lift
- Step touch
- Kicking movements
- Jack 1

The players carry out these movements rhythmically to music and carry out other movements with their hands.

DRILLS WITH A BALL

Jumping Jack
Activities
- Player A has the ball in his hands and stretches his arms forward as he opens his legs. Player B touches the ball and stretches his arms forward and backward while player A also stretches his arms forward and backward.
- The ball is transferred from hand to hand from one player to the other as they open their legs. The player who receives the ball draws it to his body as he closes his legs, then transfers it to the other player as he opens them again.
- The ball is transferred back and forth as above, but this time it is thrown parallel to the ground from one player to the other instead of being transferred from hand to hand.
- As above, only this time the players bounce the ball to each other.

Jumping Jack with ball transfer from hand to hand

Jumping Jack, bouncing the ball from player to player

Kicking movements. The players move their legs back and forth as they would for a shot at goal. They try to do this in time to the music. The most difficult aspect is coordinating the arm and foot movements.

Kicking movements while throwing the ball (1)

Kicking movements while throwing the ball (2)

Step back with ball transfer. The players can carry out typical aerobic steps while transferring the ball (throw or bounce). They can step (lunge) back or to the side or forward.

Starting position for lunge (1)

Lunge with ball transfer (2)

Drill with three balls

Each player has a ball with which he carries out tap movements. At the same time the two players carry out activities with a third ball.

Activities
- Touch the ball
- Transfer the ball back and forth
- Throw the ball back and forth
- Bounce the ball back and forth (possibly while counting to eight or four)

Throwing the ball back and forth

Other types of drills

Leg movement variations (can also be carried out in groups of two). The ball is positioned between the player's feet. He touches it with the tip of his foot or moves it a short distance to the side.

Passing back and forth along the ground. If the players pass the ball back and forth along the ground, each is forced to play the ball accurately to the other. Accompanying movements can be carried out, such as two-footed hops or low kicks.

Variations
- The ball can be passed clockwise or counterclockwise around a triangle or square.
- Group drills with several balls are very demanding. Three balls are passed clockwise or counterclockwise around a triangle. The players have to play each ball accurately and be ready to receive and control the next ball. One player counts (with or without music) and gives the start command.

Passing the ball around a triangle. The ball is dropped from the hand and kicked with the inside of the foot.

FINAL COMMENTS

You have now read through this practical book and have learned about a lot of new coaching drills. You will certainly have come across new ideas on general and soccer-specific coordination conditioning that you can put into practice in your coaching sessions. Have you already tried some of the drills? Good. Many of the organizational forms are only intended to provide a starting point - the rest is up to you. You can combine and vary the elements described in this book as you wish and experiment with your own ideas. You will be surprised how many variations occur to you once you start with coordination conditioning. I know this from my own experience.

If you have some difficulties at first, just proceed slowly step by step. Try out the easiest drills first, then try to steadily extend your repertoire of conditioning drills. If you are not sure about a drill, try it out. The value of some drills often first becomes apparent in actual practice.

Coaches of young players will certainly recognize the necessity of selective coordination conditioning. They will soon put the drills into practice. However, this book is also aimed at coaches of high school, college and professional clubs. Some of the drills are so demanding that even professionals find them challenging.

I wish all my readers lots of fun in trying out, using, varying and combining the drills described in this book.

Peter Schreiner

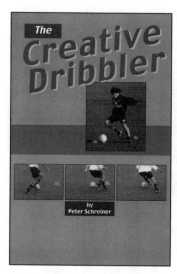

#256: The Creative Dribbler
by Peter Schreiner

Videos by Peter Schreiner

#228 Coordination, Agility and
Speed Training for Soccer
by Peter Schreiner
$34.95 Each • 2 Tape Set for $59.95

#900
SOCCEROBICS
by Peter Schreiner
$29.95

**#267 Developing
Soccer Players The
Dutch Way
$12.95**

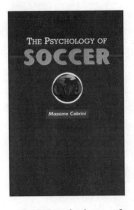

**#262 Psychology of
Soccer**
by Massimo Cabrini
$12.95

**#905 Soccer
Strategies: Defensive
and Attacking Tactics**
by Robyn Jones
$12.95

#287 Team Building
*by Kormelink and
Seeverens*
$9.95

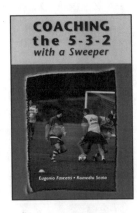

**#793 Coaching the
5-3-2 with a Sweeper**
by Fascetti and Scaia
$14.95

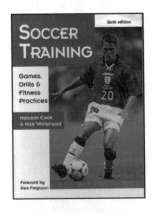

**#167 Soccer Training
Games, Drills and
Fitness Practices**
by Malcolm Cook
$14.95

**REEDSWAIN
1-800-331-5191
www.reedswain.com**

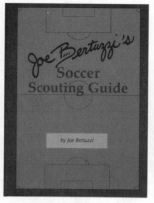

#785 Complete Book of Soccer Restart Plays
by Mario Bonfanti and Angelo Pereni
$14.95

#789 Soccer Scouting Guide
by Joe Bertuzzi
$12.95

#284 The Dutch Coaching Notebook
$14.95

#765 Attacking Schemes and Training Exercises
by Fascetti and Scaia
$14.95

#185 Conditioning for Soccer
Dr. Raymond Verheijen
$19.95

#786 Soccer Nutrition
by Enrico Arcelli
$10.95

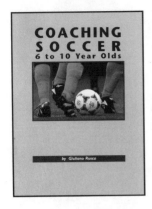

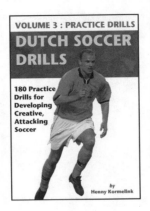

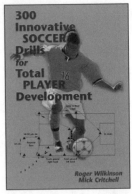

**#264 Coaching Soccer
6 to 10 year Olds**
by Giuliano Rusca
$14.95

**#195
Dutch Soccer Drills Vol. 3**
by Henny Kormelink
$12.95

**#188 300 Innovative
SOCCER Drills for
Total PLAYER
Development**
*by Roger Wilkinson
and Mick Critchell*
$14.95

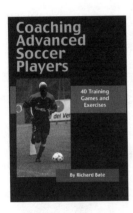

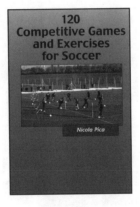

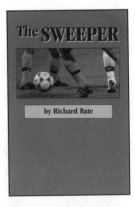

**#169 Coaching
Advanced Soccer
Players**
by Richard Bate
$12.95

**#792 120
Competitive Games
and Exercises for
Soccer**
by Nicola Pica
$14.95

#225 The Sweeper
by Richard Bate
$9.95

**REEDSWAIN
1-800-331-5191
www.reedswain.com**